DATE			

DISCARD

TRANSCULTURAL COUNSELING

New Vistas in Counseling Series

Series Editors—Garry Walz and Libby Benjamin
In collaboration with **ERIC** *Counseling and Personnel Services Information Center*

Structured Groups for Facilitating Development: Acquiring Life Skills, Resolving Life Themes, and Making Life Transitions, Volume 1
Knott, J. E., Ph.D. and Drum, D. J., Ph.D.

New Methods for Delivering Human Services, Volume 2
Jones, G. B., Ph.D., Dayton, C., Ph.D. and Gelatt, H. B., Ph.D.

Systems Change Strategies in Educational Settings, Volume 3
Arends, R. I., Ph.D. and Arends, J. H., Ph.D.

Counseling Older Persons: Careers, Retirement, Dying, Volume 4
Sinick, D., Ph.D.

Parent Education and Elementary Counseling, Volume 5
Lamb, J. and Lamb, W., Ph.D.

Counseling in Correctional Environments, Volume 6
Bennett, L. A., Ph.D., Rosenbaum, T. S., Ph.D. and McCullough, W. R., Ph.D.

Transcultural Counseling: Needs, Programs and Techniques, Volume 7
Walz, J., Ph.D., Benjamin, L., Ph.D., et al.

Career Resource Centers, Volume 8
Meerbach, J., Ed.D.

Behavior Modification Handbook for Helping Professionals, Volume 9
Mehrabian, A., Ph.D.

TRANSCULTURAL COUNSELING:
Needs, Programs, and Techniques

Edited by

Garry R. Walz, Ph.D.
Professor of Education, The University of Michigan, Ann Arbor

Libby Benjamin, Ph.D.
Associate Director of ERIC, at The University of Michigan, Ann Arbor

*Vol. 7 in the New Vistas in Counseling
Series, in collaboration with ERIC Counseling
and Personnel Services Information Center
Series Editors—Garry R. Walz and Libby Benjamin*

 **HUMAN SCIENCES PRESS**
72 Fifth Avenue   3 Henrietta Street
NEW YORK, NY 10011 ● LONDON, WC2E 8LU

Library of Congress Catalog Number 77-26253

ISBN: 0-87705-320-0

Copyright© 1978 by Human Sciences Press
72 Fifth Avenue, New York, New York 10011

Copyright is claimed until 1983. Thereafter, all portions of the work covered by
this copyright will be in the public domain. This work was developed under a
contract with the National Institute of Education, Department of Health, Education, and Welfare. However, the content does not necessarily reflect the position
or policy of that agency, and no United States Government endorsement of these
materials should be inferred.

Printed in the United States of America
89 987654321

Library of Congress Cataloging in Publication Data

Main entry under title:

Transcultural counseling.

    (New vistas in counseling; v. 7)
    Bibliography
     1. Psychiatry, Transcultural.   2. Counseling.
I. Walz, Garry Richard. II. Benjamin, Libby.
III. Series.
RC455.4.E8T69   616.8'914   77-26253
ISBN 0-87705-320-0

CONTENTS

5

FOREWORD

Developing this publication was highly rewarding for us—first, because we knew from our ERIC users how much such a document was needed, but also, and just as important, because it gave us the opportunity to talk with and get to know, albeit via telephone, so many knowledgeable, informed, and genuinely nice people.

Art Ruiz made us laugh in our very first encounter, and his breezy, unique letters were a joy always. His understanding and knowledge of the needs of Spanish-speaking peoples is profound, and we believe that he and his co-authors have written one of the most substantive and fact-filled chapters, in totally digestable style, that we have had the privilege of including in a volume of this kind.

Bill Richards had a tough task—conditions change so fast in Alaska that almost before he finished a page a new group or a new thrust emerged, and he consulted all the way with native leaders so as to insure that his chapter would be timely and true for a very unique group of clients.

We were pleased that William David Smith consented to write for us, and we believe you will hear the voice of the black American in what he has to say about the needs of his people. His suggestions will be helpful to all who counsel black clients, but the authenticity and the tone are what truly impressed us.

Joyce Chick is an old friend. We knew of the fine work she was doing in training professionals to counsel effectively with persons of other races and cultures. Her rationale for and detailed design of a training experience will be a valuable guide for persons wishing to implement such programs.

Clell Warriner takes us the next step by sharing with us in easy-to-read informal style what counselors can actually do in a group setting to facilitate harmonious transcultural relationships. Beginning with a statement on the preparation of the leader, the author presents a rationale for the group process and discusses the various kinds of groups, devoting the major share of the chapter to group themes and techniques that counselors can immediately adopt and use in their own setting. A discussion of errors commonly made by group leaders and some helpful hints for would-be facilitators conclude the chapter.

A program in transcultural group counseling with high school students is described by Dick Strub, which provides our monograph with an actual case study. Particularly helpful, we think, is the section on evaluation, which contains both objective responses from the participants, administrators, and faculty, as well as nonquantified reactions. Persons involved in conducting such group experiences will find a ready-made evaluation form included in the Appendix that they can use as is, or adapt to their particular needs.

Carol Jaslow, being on our staff, was able to delve deep into the ERIC system for descriptions of worthy programs of several kinds, and presents them to you for examination and reflection. All respond to the need for extensive changes in guidance services delivered to persons of differing cultural and ethnic minority backgrounds. We wanted to conclude this monograph with a sampling of different kinds of efforts so that readers could be assured that progress *is* being made in attempts to provide useful, impactful programs in this neglected field.

Taken together, we believe that this compilation of documents can be a most helpful resource for persons who sincerely wish to devote their energies to making the world a place where all of us can live and work together in tranquility and peace.

Garry R. Walz and Libby Benjamin
Director and Associate Director, ERIC/CAPS

Chapter 1

ISSUES IN THE COUNSELING OF SPANISH-SPEAKING/SURNAMED CLIENTS: RECOMMENDATIONS FOR THERAPEUTIC SERVICES

Rene A. Ruiz
Amado M. Padilla
Rodolfo Alvarez

This chapter discusses issues of ethnic identification and marginal assimilation, demographic characteristics of the Spanish-speaking/surnamed (SSS) groups, the pattern of utilization of counseling services by the SSS, the factors that reduce self-referrals, and typical problems SSS clients bring to counseling—problems different from and often greater than the life problems experienced by other Americans. The concluding portion of the chapter is devoted to recommendations for the delivery of more effective counseling services to the SSS.

Successful counseling depends upon effective communication between counselor and client. The counselor must comprehend the needs and problems of the client, and the client must understand messages from the counselor. These messages are designed to help the client achieve

Work on this paper was supported by the Spanish-Speaking Mental Health Research and Development Program at UCLA; R. Alvarez, Principal Investigator, NIHM Grant MH-24845-02.

greater self-actualization and self-reliance as a means of ultimately increasing his or her capacity to function productively in society, and these goals cannot be met if the messages are not understood. The precise purposes of this chapter are to provide background information and techniques that will enable counselors to communicate more effectively and to counsel more successfully with Spanish-speaking/surnamed (SSS) clients. To achieve these goals, we present comments organized around the following themes: (1) issues of ethnic identification and marginal assimilation; (2) demographic characteristics of the SSS group; (3) a review of the utilization pattern of counseling services by the target population; (4) an examination of factors operating to reduce self-referrals from the SSS; and (5) several case histories which illustrate the kinds of problems and complaints SSS clients typically bring to counseling. In this last section we attempt to demonstrate how the issues and events presented in the four preceding sections tend to create a pattern of life problems that are different from and exclusive of the life problems experienced by other Americans. Simultaneously, we attempt to sensitize counselors to how SSS clients are different. In the concluding section we offer recommendations for the delivery of more effective counseling services to the SSS.

Several final comments seem appropriate to orient the reader to the direction and emphasis of the chapter. The realm of services subsumed under counseling is extremely broad. A partial listing includes the use of counseling techniques (sometimes including test scores) to select academic majors or vocational choice; to resolve specific problems (e.g., drug abuse, suicide prevention, and marital treatment); to facilitate personal growth (e.g., self-actualization among "normal" clients); or to treat individual psychopathology. Although we present principles that can be generalized to a variety of counseling approaches, the primary orientation of the chapter is to counseling as psychother-

apy, which is defined as a process of enhanced self-awareness leading to more efficient, productive, and satisfying
life adjustment. Furthermore, our comments are deliberately presented in the broadest terms so that they can be
adapted by a variety of counselors, regardless of whether
their theoretical orientation is psychodynamic, behavioral,
or humanistic/existential. Finally, our recommendations
for culture-specific counseling are designed to apply to all
SSS clients, regardless of subgroup differences such as nation of origin, length of residence in the United States, or
urban versus rural dwelling.

ETHNIC IDENTIFICATION AND THE MARGINAL PERSON

The assumptions which underlie this section are that everyone is a member of at least one culture, that some are
members of more than one, that the degree of commitment
to a given culture varies among multicultural persons depending upon the degree of assimilation, and that culture
group membership influences behavior. In the context of
this chapter, of course, our primary focus will be upon
those behaviors which are examined in determining
whether or not a person's overall life adjustment is normal
or healthy (Ruiz & Wrenn, in press; Wrenn & Ruiz, 1970).
Before proceeding further, however, certain key terms will
be defined.

The concept of identification, defined simply as imita-
tion of elders by the young, was already well known by the
times of the Ptolemaic and Greek philosophers. Its earliest
definition within the context of a formal theory, however,
does not appear until about 1900 among psychoanalysts.
This definition was modified even further as it was incorporated into theories of social science, especially sociology
and social psychology. Basically, contemporary usage of
the concept refers to a process, resulting in an end-state,

by which an individual assumes a pattern of behavior characteristic of other people in his environment. Originally, the child imitates the behavior of parents (called *modeling*), but subsequently models the behavior of other adults such as relatives and teachers, and of other peers such as playmates and fellow students. Through this process the child gradually acquires the behavioral repertoire of the people around him.

Although identification clearly refers to the totality of self-experience, the term *ethnic identification* refers to that part of the self which includes those values, attitudes, and preferences that comprise cultural group membership. Thus the child who speaks Spanish at home and English at school is obviously bicultural and, by our definition, experiences dual ethnic identification.

Two issues require elaboration at this point. First, we have selected language skill in this illustration as an index of culture group membership. Although we are convinced that this index is valid, we also recognize the existence of other equally valid criteria; custom, tradition, law, religion, costume, dietary preference, and so on. Thus, although language skill serves to make the point, one must examine a number of variables in determining the ethnic identification of a given client. Our second point is that bicultural group membership creates the *potential,* but not necessarily the actual experience of divided group loyalty and confusion about the self. This latter point is extremely important and should be kept in mind while examining sections relative to treatment—especially the case histories and the section of recommendations for SSS counseling.

The term *marginal person* stems primarily from the work of Stonequist (1937), and denotes bicultural membership combined with the relative inability to form dual ethnic identification. This is a complex theoretical statement and one with significant implications for effective communication and successful counseling of the SSS. To maximize the clarity of our message, we illustrate the subsequent discussion with references to the target population.

Most SSS are bicultural as we have defined the term. That is, they hold simultaneous membership in two different cultural groups—the Anglo dominant majority and their particular SSS minority subgroup. (The inference of bicultural membership is documented, and the various SSS subgroups are identified in the section on utilization of services.) Two points are relevant here. First, bicultural membership and dual ethnic identification are in no sense intrinsically pathologic. One may argue quite cogently, for example, that multicultural group membership is a normal or expected state of affairs. This is not to imply that we are all multiethnic, but rather that we all belong to a multitude of groups with different values and attitudes. One person may be a practicing Catholic and be committed to the women's liberation movement, a second may be Catholic but uninterested in women's liberation, a third may be a Lutheran and committed to women's liberation, and so on.

Our second point is implied in the preceding example. The degree of commitment to cultural values varies. To return to the discussion of ethnic identification, degree of commitment may vary from strong to weak. This continuum of commitment appears as a two-by-two matrix in Table 1–1.

Table 1–1. Degree of Ethnic Identification Among Bicultural SSS Americans

| | | The Majority Anglo Culture | |
		Strong	Weak
The Minority	Strong	A	B
SSS Culture	Weak	D	C

Note that individuals in cell A would manifest strong commitments to two cultures—the Anglo dominant majority and their own particular SSS subgroup. Continuing to use language as an index of ethnic identification, one would predict both fluent English and Spanish. On the basis of strong commitment to two different cultures, one would anticipate a minimum of problems associated with bicultural group membership or ethnic identification. Clients from cell A seeking counseling would probably present problems manifested in the area of personal life adjustment relatively independent of their ethnic group membership.

Now consider individuals in cells B and D. Cell B people manifest a strong commitment to the traditional value system of their minority culture and a weak one to the majority group. Continuing to use language skill for illustrative purposes, one would predict that fluency in Spanish would surpass English. In cell D, of course, the situation would be reversed. Individuals in these two cells may or may not bring problems to the counselor which are related to ethnic identification. The individual in transition from one culture to another, that is, deliberately attempting to replace one set of cultural values by another, may be experiencing problems in ethnic identification. The Spanish dominant person who is attempting to enter the majority culture by acquiring English fluency, as well as the English dominant individual who is trying to regain contact with his cultural heritage by learning Spanish, will probably experience stress associated with culture change. But it is very important to note that his or her source of stress does not apply unless the individual is in the process of transition from one culture to another. The SSS who have a strong commitment to one culture and a weak commitment to another, and who are comfortable with this situation, appear unlikely to present problems in ethnic identification.

People in cell C seem to represent the "failures" of cells B and D—that is, they have surrendered their original commitment, whether minority or majority, but have not yet successfully entered their newly chosen culture. Some individuals, for example, might minimize Spanish usage in social interaction to appear more "American." If this occurs before the acquisition of English fluency, of course, comprehension may be limited, and they will be forced to remain relatively silent in many situations, or appear ludicrous. If one generalizes this example to the abandonment of one set of cultural values before the acquisition of an alternative set, one can envision a variety of situations in which the marginal person cannot cope efficiently with the stress of ordinary day-to-day life because the values, attitudes, and social relationships of the original culture have been left behind. Imagine the intensity of discomfort experienced when a marginal person leaves one culture, tries to enter another, is not fully accepted, and is left in limbo between two different, and sometimes conflicting, value systems.

THE TARGET POPULATION

This section presents selected data to demonstrate how the SSS are like, and different from, other Americans.

Population

The United States Census of 1971 presents and reports separately data on persons of Spanish origin. Broken down by country of national origin, the distribution of the total population of 9,073,600 appears in Table 1–2.

Area of Residence

The 1971 census also reveals that geographic area of residence is related to ethnicity. For example, 87% of the Mexican Americans reside in the southwest United States (California, Texas, Arizona, New Mexico, and Colorado); 76% of the Puerto Ricans reside in New York, New Jersey,

Table 1–2. U.S. Population of Spanish Origin,
Subdivided by Country of Origin

Country of Origin	Totals (in millions)
Central–South America	0.5
Cuba	0.6
Mexico	5.0
Puerto Rico	1.5
Other	1.4
Totals	9.0

Adapted from a table with a similar title in: Selected characteristics of persons and families of Mexican, Puerto Rican, and other Spanish origin: March, 1971. U.S. Bureau of the Census, *Current Population Reports*, Series P–20, No. 224. Washington, D.C.: U.S. Government Printing Office, 1972, p. 3.

or Connecticut; and most Cubans live in Florida. Furthermore, the vast majority of the SSS dwells in urban areas; 82.5% compared to 67.8% for the total population and to 76.0% for blacks.

Income

The 1971 census reported that 2.4 million SSS (26.7%) were classified as living in "poverty." Two years later, 21.9% of the SSS were placed in a category described as "low income." These percentage differences over this period seem to suggest an increased standard of living, but the conclusion is uncertain because criteria for inclusion in the two categories are unavailable and it is unknown whether the effect of inflation was considered. In any event, when one considers that 21.9% of the SSS in 1973 were in the low income category compared to 11.1% of the general population, it is clear that the relative proportion of SSS poor, to poor who are non-SSS, is about two to one.

The inference that the standard of living among the SSS is relatively lower is supported by examination of census data on personal and family income (1970–1973). In 1970 the median income for SSS males was $6,220 compared to $8,220 in the general population. The distribution of family income in 1973 appears in Table 1–3.

Table 1–3.   U.S. Family Income
Among General and SSS Population

Family Income	General Population	SSS Families
Under $5,000	14.7%	23.0%
$5,000 to $10,000	23.3%	35.0%
$10,000 to $15,000	25.5%	23.7%
Over $15,000	35.5%	18.4%

Employment

The finding that personal and family income among the SSS is lower than the national average suggests that the SSS are probably overrepresented in menial and lower-paying occupations. And, in fact, it is true that they are. More than 56% of the SSS are employed in blue-collar jobs. SSS males were employed most commonly in transportation and/or as operators—for example, gas station attendants, produce packers, drillers, and manufacturing checkers. The second most common form of employment was as craftsmen, such as repairmen, machinists, and furniture finishers. For SSS women, clerical and operative jobs were the most common.

Lower annual income and overrepresentation in menial occupations may be assumed to be associated with lower rates of employment, and this is exactly what one finds. A report by the Bureau of Labor Statistics identified 325,000 unemployed SSS during the third quarter of 1974. This figure represents an unemployment rate of 8.0% for the SSS, which is higher than the national level (5.0%), but lower than the black rate (10.5%). These figures are even more ominous than they appear, however, because they reflect an annual increase in unemployment of 29% for the SSS, compared to an increase of 22% among the general population and 8% among blacks.

Education

Low-income and menial work may be assumed to inter-correlate with limited education; and once again, the census data confirm this expectation. The U.S. census of 1969 recorded that, as of November of that year, the median years of education among SSS who were 25 and older was 9.3, compared to 12.2 for the general population and 9.6 for blacks. In this same age group, 19.5% of the SSS had completed less than 5 years of school, compared to 5.0% for the general population and 13.5% for blacks. Within the same age group the percentages that finished high school were 32.6% for the SSS, 56.4% for the general population, and 34.7% for blacks. Thus by three criteria— median years of education, percentage with less than 5 years of school, and percentage completing high school— the SSS receive less education compared either to the general population or to blacks.

Language

The 1969 census also reported the retention of Spanish fluency; 68.9% of the SSS identify Spanish as their mother tongue, while only 28.8% identify English. Within the total population, Spanish has a base rate preference of 3.4%, while the preference for English is 81.6%. Mother tongue preferences do not add up to 100% because of a category entitled "other [mother tongue] and not reported," which equals 2.3% among the SSS and 15% among the total population. Among the SSS, 48.7% report that Spanish is usually spoken in the home, while 50.3% prefer to speak English. In the total population English is preferred to

Spanish by 94.1% compared to 2.3%. Once again, totals approximate but do not add up to 100% because of other language preferences and unreported data.

Cultural Diversity

We believe that the SSS are culturally heterogeneous, and we are particularly explicit in this argument because at least two sources of information may mislead the unsophisticated reader into the erroneous inference that the SSS comprise a single, unified, and homogeneous culture group. First, we have summarized census data which, by its very nature, tend to gloss over significant differences among subculture groups. With the exception of the fact that SSS subgroups tend to distribute themselves in different geographic regions as a function of national origin, the global nature of the data reported implies that all SSS are alike. Second, the common history of Spanish heritage and all the similarities such as language, religion and custom, also support the mistaken inference of cultural homogeneity. However a more careful look at these SSS subgroups shows that the cultural differences are greater than the similarities.

First, the different SSS subgroups arrived in this nation at different times. Exploration from Mexico began in 1528 with the crossing of the Rio Grande, and migration continues to the present day. Within the last few decades, relatively large numbers of Cubans and Puerto Ricans have immigrated to the United States and have thus enlarged the SSS pool. Second, people left their homes for a variety of reasons: exploration, colonization, economic opportunity, and personal liberty. Third, genetic differences distinguish the various SSS subgroups. Spaniards in Mexico intermarried with native inhabitants, and their progeny formed an ethnic group which created a new Indo-Hispanic culture. In other parts of the New World, especially Puerto Rico and some areas of South America, natives were slain or driven off, and the indigenous cultures were lost. To create a pool of cheap labor, slaves from Africa were imported. In the course of time, new cultures were formed on the basis of influences from the New World, Europe, and Africa. The net result is that some SSS subgroups display marked differences in skin color, ranging from European "white," through mulatto skin tones, to African "black."

Other factors create or maintain cultural differences among the various SSS subgroups upon their arrival in the United States. Considering the long-standing American prejudice against dark skin color, for example, it should come as no surprise that black SSS are treated differently from white SSS. Differential treatment, of course, would tend to isolate the two groups even more.

Differences in employment skills also tend to insulate some SSS groups from others. Many Cubans, for example, arrived in the United States fluent in both Spanish and English, with professional degrees and an urban background including familiarity with industrial technology. These people are obviously quite different from recent Puerto Rican immigrants who tend to be monolingual-Spanish, with fewer years of formal education, and from a rural-agricultural background.

Conclusions

Data summarized in this section support the following conclusions: (1) The SSS are a numerically large ethnic minority group, second in size only to blacks. (2) The SSS consist of at least five major subgroups based on national origin alone. (3) The SSS are largely urban, but geographic distribution by state(s) of residence is a function of ethnicity. (4) The SSS suffer from the effects of the "poverty cycle"—low individual and family income, overrepresentation in menial and low-paying occupations, higher rates of unemployment, and fewer years of formal education. (5) The SSS demonstrate a higher rate of bilingualism than other Americans. The various SSS subgroups are members of uniquely different cultures. The last point, that the SSS vary among themselves with regard to ethnic identification, will be of maximal importance in utilizing an appropriate counseling approach for a given SSS client.

UTILIZATION OF SERVICES

This section reviews the literature indicating that the SSS under-utilize available counseling services.

Rates of Use

A review of the scant literature indicates that the SSS have been seriously underrepresented among the clientele of existing mental health services facilities. For example, Karno and Edgerton (1969), using California census figures, estimated that Mexican Americans made up 9–10% of the state's population in 1962–1963. They found that during this same period the percentages of Mexican Americans admitted for treatment in Californian facilities were as follows: 2.2% to the state hospital system, 3.4% to state mental hygiene clinics, 0.9% to the Neuropsychiatric Institute, and 2.3% to state and local facilities. The resident inpatient population was 3.3%. Thus underrepresentation ranges from 6.6% to 9.1%.

The situation is similar in other geographic locales. For example, Jaco (1960), in a survey of the incidence of mental disorders from 1951 to 1952 in Texas, also reported lower utilization of private and public mental hospitals by Mexican Americans. A similar under-utilization of a university's counseling services by Chicano students has recently been reported in an unpublished manuscript by Perez (1975).

A comprehensive and extensive report has recently been published which documents a distressingly similar picture of underutilization in state and county mental hospitals across the nation (Bachrach, 1975). This report presents a wealth of data which are invaluable for the counselor seriously interested in the delivery of valid services to the SSS. The major points for our purposes are these: (1) The age-adjusted rate of admissions for the SSS is 155 per 100,000 population, compared to 181 for other whites and 334 for nonwhites. (2) The age-adjusted admission rates are approximately double for SSS males compared to SSS females (212 to 103 per 100,000 population). (3) When figures are adjusted for population differences, SSS admissions are relatively youthful, and they are higher than other white admissions rates in the age group 14 to 25 years.[1] (4). The highest age-specific admissions rate is found among the SSS aged (65 years and older), with a rate of 278 per 100,000 population compared to 127 and 259 for whites and nonwhites.

Elsewhere we have suggested that although the SSS receive comparatively less mental health care than the general population, they actually need more (Padilla & Ruiz, 1973; Padilla, Ruiz, & Alvarez, 1975). One reason for this is that most of the SSS are only partially acculturated and marginally integrated economically. As a consequence they face disadvantages known to be correlated with personality disintegration and subsequent need for treatment intervention, including (1) poor communication skills in English; (2) the poverty cycle—limited education, lower

---

[1]The elevated utilization rate among SSS between the ages of 14 and 25 may be accounted for by their higher rate of drug disorders— 23 per 100,000 population—than for other whites and nonwhites, who had respective rates of 8 and 19 (Bachrach, 1975).

income, depressed social status, deteriorated housing, and minimal political influence; (3) the survival of traits from a rural agrarian culture that are relatively ineffectual in an urban technological society; (4) the necessity of seasonal migration (for some); and (5) the very stressful problem of acculturation to a society that appears prejudicial, hostile, and rejecting. Accordingly, we conclude that demographic data underestimate the frequency and severity of factors impinging upon the mental health of the SSS, and that the under-utilization of mental health services by this population is therefore even more crucial than we know. The latter conclusion is particularly telling since a wide range of mental health modalities does not seem to be as available for the SSS as it does for other U.S. citizens.

FACTORS REDUCING SELF-REFERRAL

In this section we review factors that reduce the utilization of available counseling services by the SSS.

DISCOURAGING INSTITUTIONAL POLICIES

Certain organizational factors and institutional policies are primarily responsible for the utilization patterns of mental health facilities by the SSS. A review of the literature by Gordon (1965), who was concerned with characteristics of patients seeking treatment at child guidance clinics, suggests that the needs of minority group children are not being met (cited by Wolkon et al., 1974). Primary factors responsible for this situation are defined as "inflexible intake procedures and long waiting lists." A study of a specific child guidance clinic confirmed the inference based on the literature review (Wolkon et al., 1974). The period between the initial self-referral for service and the intake interview ranged from 1 to 52 weeks, with a median of 28 weeks. The four Mexican American families seeking treatment had a median wait of 28 weeks with a range of 24.5 to 42.5 weeks. In emergencies patients were seen "immediately." At the same clinic the median waiting period for Caucasians was only 4.5 weeks, whereas the Mexican Americans had to wait 5.5 weeks. Although these differences are not statistically significant, it is clear that an emergency telephone contact is not generally honored for more than a month in the case of Caucasians, but it takes almost 6 weeks in the case of Mexican Americans. The inference that delays for ordinary and emergency treatment are discouraging is confirmed by the finding that "77% of the total initial request for services did not receive treatment."

A study even more directly relevant to treatment of the SSS (Torrey, 1972) describes mental health facilities located in a cachement area of one million persons, of whom approximately 100,000 are Mexican American. Torrey evaluates these facilities as "irrelevant" for Mexican Americans because 10% of the local population generates only 4% of the patient referrals. The basis of his judgment is that the bilingual poor should be expected to generate a larger proportion of referrals because they are subject to many stresses known to bring on mental breakdown. His explanation for this discrepancy is based primarily on the following four variables: geographic isolation, language barriers, class-bound values, and culture-bound values.

Geographic Isolation

Mental health services are "inaccessible" because they are often located as far as possible from the neighborhood of the group with the highest need. All too often community mental health services are attached to schools of medicine or universities located outside of the barrio and accessible only by a bus ride that is time consuming and accompanied by various social difficulties. Not only does the distance impede the frequency-of self-referrals, but both the cost of transportation and the lack of adequate child care during the absence of the mother also serve to decrease the utilization of mental health facilities by the SSS.

Language Barriers

Torrey describes the majority of local Mexican Americans as bilingual and a "significant minority as speaking little or no English." Nevertheless, only five members of a professional staff of 120 studied by Torrey spoke any Spanish at all, and none of the directional and/or instructional signs were in Spanish. The interpretation that referrals will decrease if patient and therapist cannot communicate is shared by Edgerton and Karno (1971) and by Karno and Edgerton (1969), among others.

Class-Bound Values

Here the reference is primarily to therapist variables, that is, to the personal characteristics of the professional staff that dissuade the patient from continued mental health treatment. Abad et al. (1974), Yamamoto et al. (1968), and Torrey (1972) all indicate that therapists conduct treatment in accordance with the value system of the middle class—the client is seen individually or in a group for 50 minutes once or twice a week. This approach has proven ineffective with and discouraging to lower-class patients. Frustrated because clients fail to respond to this approach, counselors discouraged clients from seeking continued therapy after the first meeting. These points have also been noted by the Karno-Edgerton group and by Kline (1969).

Culture-Bound Values

Again, Torrey (1972) attends to therapist variables. He posits that whenever therapists from one culture diagnose and prescribe treatment for patients from another culture, there is an inherent probability of professional misjudgment. To illustrate, he cites data indicating that 90% of Anglo residents in psychiatry associate the phrase, "hears voices," with the word, "crazy," whereas only 16% of Mexican American high school students make the same association. The concept of intrinsic culture conflict is also advanced by Bloombaum, Yamamoto, and James (1968); the Karno-Edgerton group; Kline (1969); and Phillipus (1971).

Conclusions

Although all four factors operated to minimize self-referrals to mental health centers by the SSS, the last three (language, class, and culture) seem to interact in such a way that the SSS are largely discouraged from utilizing mental health services. A review of studies of low-income patients, both white and nonwhite, who apply for mental health services is particularly relevant here (Lorion, 1973). One major conclusion that emerges from this review is that middle-class therapists are typically members of a different cultural group than are low-class patients. As a consequence, patient and therapist experience all the difficulties in communication which occur whenever members of two cultures interact. This "culture conflict" is described in much greater detail in a second paper by the same author (Lorion, 1974). Therapists, and particularly therapists in training, tend to be "turned off" by low-income patients because the patients are perceived as hostile, suspicious people who use crude language and expect merely symptomatic relief.

Studies reviewed by Lorion reveal that the success of a therapist in working with low-income patients is attributable more to the personal characteristics of the therapists than to their experience level or treatment approach. Lorion also reports that therapists from low socioeconomic backgrounds are equally successful with patients from all social classes. However the reverse does not seem to be true: Upper class therapists cannot deal with equal effectiveness across social classes. More interesting is the fact that low-income patients engage in significantly more self-exploration early in treatment if their therapist is of the same race and/or socioeconomic background. Cobb (1972), in a review of similar literature, supports an argument made earlier in this article that therapeutic expectations vary to some extent as a function of social class. Patients of low socioeconomic status seem to expect therapists to assume a more active role, as physicians typically do in dealing with medical problems, rather than a passive or talking role. As a result, Cobb concludes that such patients will probably respond better to therapists who are more active.

Taken together, these authors (Cobb, 1972; Lorion, 1973, 1974) agree that the race and social class of the therapist affect the patient's response to treatment. Thus it seems reasonable to infer that an effective and appropriate "solution" to a problem, proposed by a white, middle-class counselor and based upon middle-class values, may be inappropriate and ineffective for a patient coming from, and returning to, his lower-class environment.

CASE HISTORIES

In this section we present a series of autobiographical statements, accompanied by our observations and comments, compiled from case histories of SSS clients seeking help. We have taken two steps to preserve the anonymity of these clients: We withhold all information concerning the source of these case histories, and we have drastically altered any information that might identify the client.

These case histories are introduced to sensitize the counselor to the unique aspects of the problems presented by SSS clients. To varying degrees the effect upon life adjustment of socioeconomic factors such as the poverty cycle is illustrated. At a more subtle level of analysis, note how some of the chief complaints may be conceptualized as maladaptive responses to societal stress, whereas others appear to reflect personal problems in adjustment. Maria, for example, is clearly experiencing problems in ethnic identification (Spanish versus Chicana), and she is, in certain regards, a marginal person. Aside from that, available information suggests that her overall life adjustment is satisfactory. Antonio, on the other hand, has clearly made a strong commitment to Chicano culture and has thus reduced problems in ethnic identification or marginality. He seems to be what we termed earlier a "cell B" person (see Figure 1.1). His personal judgment and social skills are so poor, however, that he is in constant trouble with his parents, neighbors, and the police. Reynaldo manifests both societal and personal problems in adjustment. In reading these three case histories, attempt to discriminate between societal and intrapsychic sources of stress, and begin to formulate counseling programs based upon information available to you.

Case 1: Maria

This first statement was elicited from a young woman whose ancestors had resided in northern New Mexico for generations. In that area, self-attributed ethnic identification among the SSS is commonly described as *Hispano* in Spanish or as *Spanish American* in English. Maria had lived in relative sociocultural isolation until she moved to California to attend junior college. There, for the first time, she encountered Chicanos and Chicanas who were more liberated, political, and assertive. Maria was treated with scorn, suspicion, and even hostility when she described herself to SSS classmates as Spanish American rather than Chicana. But her greatest shock came in trying to adjust to new behavioral norms in the absence of the emotional support and guidance customarily provided by her parents, family, and friends at home. Here are her words.

> Moving away from home had a great psychological impact on me and my ideals. I had some difficulty adjusting myself to a completely new and independent form of life. Being Spanish American, I was always closely bound to the family. When I tried to deviate from the norm, I was reprimanded and reminded of the obligation I had to the family. Living away from home taught me to appreciate them [the family] and their conservative values more than I had before. . . . But we sure are different from the people in California!

At the time that Maria sought counseling, she could not completely verbalize these disturbing incompatibilities between her cultural upbringing and that of her peers. Who was she? Was she Spanish as her family had told her, or was she Chicana as her friends insisted? How involved should she become in the Chicano movement? She brought these questions to her counselor. These are difficult counseling problems for one who is sophisticated and knowledgeable, but much more difficult for anyone unfamiliar with the historical context in which Maria was reared.

Case 2: Antonio

Blinded by a belief that he is destined to become a great Chicano leader, Antonio (he hates to be called Tony) is a member of every Chicano organization in his community and attends every Chicano function within a 200-mile radius of his home. He is so active politically he rarely attends class, and has difficulty keeping a job because of absenteeism or arguments with Anglo coworkers. He has become a nuisance on elementary school playgrounds where he tries to instruct his "little brothers and sisters" in Chicano culture. But Antonio is a grown man in his late twenties. His appearance is unusual for his neighborhood—he wears denim jackets with embroidered political slogans and his long hair is held back with a decorated leather thong in "Indian" fashion. Parents and school officials have expressed concern about his loitering near playgrounds, and the police have questioned and warned Antonio more than once. Listen to Antonio as he refers to his ethnic identification and decide for yourself the nature of his problem.

> Because of Mexican American descent my parents wish to see their son attend college or university and further the Chicano cause. We speak Spanish frequently at home and maintain the Mexican heritage. We are a proud family—of our home, community, and heritage. I wish to become something proud, an example to my thousands of little brothers and sisters in the barrios across the nation.

Clearly, Antonio has a problem. His parents are pressuring him to become more conscientious in college and work, and to be less active politically. Social relations have become strained with neighbors, school officials, and police. Obviously, Antonio agrees he needs help since he referred himself for counseling. His presenting complaint is that "people do not understand." He is quite insensitive to his impact on others, but his low insight does not appear psychotic. How could you counsel Antonio? Do you think he would respond differently to an Anglo or Chicano counselor? How could family and community support systems be mobilized to facilitate improved adjustment for Antonio?

Case 3: Reynaldo

Reynaldo is a young man, obviously bright and ambitious. His motivation is to become an "intellectual," but he has not yet decided upon a course of study. His college education is being delayed sómewhat because he typically responds to evaluative situations, such as course exams, with attacks of anxiety accompanied by outbursts of nonspecific somatic symptomatology. He has been hospitalized on several occasions, but fairly extensive workups have failed to reveal any organic pathology. Reynaldo referred himself for treatment at the Student Counseling Center because of a burgeoning recognition that his anxiety and hypochondriasis are psychogenic. Here is a statement he made during a group counseling session with Anglo and SSS clients.

> My parents are native Spanish speakers, with limited English fluency. My English is much better than theirs, which really helps out in school. They have encouraged my college education and with their financial support I will make it through, but it won't be easy. I'm dedicated to school. I want to become an intellectual . . . to learn skills to help my people. My major problems are that I "blow up" on exams and can't show my teachers what I've learned . . . plus the fact that my doctor bills have been so high my parents are beginning to worry where the money for my tuition is coming from.

As group counseling progressed, it became clear that Reynaldo had a more serious problem in ethnic identification than these excerpted remarks reveal. He mocked the broken English of his parents, even though their English fluency was superior to his comprehension of Spanish. He scorned what he termed the "disadvantaged culture" of his parents, even though, as other SSS members of his counseling group were quick to point out, he was almost ignorant of the history, tradition, and language of his ethnic group. His strong identification with Anglo-American values and norms was recognized by his tendency to refer to other SSS as "those people."

Reynaldo's personal problems are no less severe than his confused ethnic identification. As stated earlier, he is excessively anxiety-prone and somatizes in response to stress. His self-exploration during group counseling revealed underlying feelings of personal insecurity combined with a barely recognized reluctance to assume responsibility for his own life. Fellow group members advised Reynaldo to get a job, even if only part-time, and to help pay for his school and medical expenses out of his earnings instead of depending so heavily on his parents.

You have been deliberately deprived of information concerning specific SSS subgroup membership or socioeconomic status. Reflect upon the case of Reynaldo, manipulate ethnicity and demography, and contemplate how various combinations might influence the severity of his maladjustment and the type of counseling program that would seem most appropriate. If, for example, Reynaldo were an impoverished Chicano residing in an urban barrio, his maladjustment would seem maximally severe. His relatives, neighbors, and peers would probably be bilingual and much less motivated to achieve assimilation than Reynaldo. In such an environment Reynaldo would be perceived as weird and his rejection of Chicanos and of Chicano culture would be interpreted as a personal insult and ethnic slur. It seems more likely that the familial and neighborhood response would represent some combination of social isolation and overt aggression. It appears equally likely that one goal of high priority in counseling would be to help Reynaldo understand, accept, and integrate those aspects of self he seems to be striving to deny.

Suppose, on the other hand, that Reynaldo is the offspring of an upper-class, well-educated Cuban refugee family that has deliberately decided to make the United States a permanent home.[2] Now, it seems at least possible,

---

[2]Nothing in this example or the preceding one should be misinterpreted as implying that the authors share the commonly held, but mistaken, notions that all Chicanos are impoverished and ignorant while all Cubans are wealthy and educated.

though some may disagree, that Reynaldo's attempt to assimilate may be adaptive, rather than pathologic. Considering that his adoption of new cultural values is consistent with family wishes, and remembering that loyalty and obedience to the family are highly valued SSS traits, Reynaldo's behavior appears less inappropriate. Notice further that ethnicity and socioeconomic status also influence our opinions on the degree of pathology of other behaviors. We implied quite strongly, for example, that a poor Chicano youth who expected his parents to subsidize his college education was almost certainly lacking in personal autonomy, but the same expectation in an upper-class Cuban youth might be normative. Note also that this upper-class Cuban youth is much more like an Anglo middle-class youth than a lower-class Chicano youngster.

Suppose, as a third alternative, that Reynaldo is a dark-skinned Puerto Rican from a family of moderate means. One may speculate whether there is any connection between his rejection of his SSS culture, his feelings of personal insecurity, and possible formative experiences of discrimination and prejudice. If such a connection exists—that is, if Reynaldo is trying to pretend he is white by minimizing his SSS ethnic identification—then his behavior is clearly pathologic. He is doomed to a lifetime of chronic frustration. If such a connection does not exist, then his behavior assumes a much less pathologic connotation. Like Reynaldo the Cuban, Reynaldo the Puerto Rican may be involved in a healthy transition from one culture to another. Since Reynaldo's parents have been described in this instance as having moderate financial means, it is not entirely clear whether the subsidy of Reynaldo's education would represent a hardship for the family. On the basis of the sparse information provided, it is equally difficult to determine in this instance whether Reynaldo's expectation of such support reflects excessive dependence.

RECOMMENDATIONS FOR SSS COUNSELING

As indicated earlier, we believe it is unrealistic and counter-productive to separate tips for the counselor and recommendations for institutional change in the agencies where counseling occurs. Both must go hand-in-hand if the SSS are to receive more adequate counseling services in schools, places of employment, or clinics. A comprehensive set of recommendations for institutional change in community mental health organizations appears in Alvarez et al. (1974). Below we offer recommendations for counseling improvements around seven themes. The first four of these themes pertain mostly to the organization of counseling service facilities, whereas the last three apply more directly to the individual counselor.

Access to Services

The first recommendation concerns the geographic location of the counseling services. It is logistically sound, as well as logical, to place service agencies in the neighborhood of the target population. If for any reason such a suggestion seems impossible to implement, the second preference would be to locate the agency in an area serviced by rapid, dependable, and cheap transportation. After all, many of the SSS are members of the lowest socioeconomic groups and do not own cars. It goes without saying that people who are pinching pennies to feed their children are not going to spend money on cab fare to a distant counseling agency. If the agency is far from the neighborhood of the target population and public transportation is unavailable, it becomes incumbent upon the agency to share some of the responsibility for solving the problem. To some extent locally situated storefront or outreach centers can help. Another alternative is to create a transportation system by combining a telephone call-in service, monitored by bilingual workers, with a car or bus pick-up system.

Delivery of Personal Services

While it seems unrealistic to expect a service agency to provide a cadre of counselors to wait around to offer immediate services for clientele without appointments, we suggest the creation of some mechanism whereby a client can be seen immediately if at all possible. The counseling staff might agree to schedule their time so that one or two counselors are always on call. Thus, at least theoretically, a counselor would almost always be available for immediate consultation with a walk-in client. If the entire on-call staff becomes occupied, we suggest that some form of backup service be provided for the unexpected client. The receptionist could be informed of each counselor's schedule to determine who might be available the soonest. This counselor could be notified of the situation, interrupt the ongoing counseling session if necessary, and take a minute to meet, greet, and shake hands with the new arrival. The counselor could explain to the client the attempt of the agency to provide immediate services and the nature of the current situation. The client could also be informed of the exact length of time necessary to wait for his "immediate" consultation.

In addition to the personal greeting and handshake, we also suggest self-introductions and conversation based on first names rather than on more formal titles, such as Mr., Mrs., Ms., Miss, Dr., or Nurse. These strategems are important primarily because of their demonstrated success in increasing self-referrals from the Spanish-speaking population. It is equally important however, to note how knowledge of the value system of a specific subculture can be manipulated to modify the behavior of its members. In this case the Latino preference to interact with *people* rather than *institutions*, combined with the greater importance of physical contact, is being exploited to increase the quality of counseling services delivered to the target population.

In this general context, the reader is reminded once again that most of the SSS are working-class people with a commitment to a usual work schedule of Monday through Friday, from 8:00 a.m. to 5:00 p.m., if not longer. Thus any agency operating on a congruent time schedule will automatically be open while the majority of the SSS male population is working, and will be closed when these potential clients are available. Our next recommendation emerges logically from this situation. We suggest that the counseling agency offer services during the free time of the potential clientele. This requires staying open after hours or a full work day on Saturday, but such a schedule seems necessary to serve the SSS community. Staggering work schedules—for example, serving clients from 1:00 p.m. to 9:00 p.m. rather than the usual 8:00 a.m. to 5:00 p.m.—is one effective solution that might even be more attractive to the staff.

One final suggestion concerning structural informality seems warranted, although the data base for the recommendation is impressionistic rather than experimental. Because SSS clients seem to prefer reception areas with informal decor, we suggest that counselors consider furnishing their treatment space like a family room or den— with sofas, chairs, rugs, pictures, and live plants—rather than like a more traditional office with a desk, chair on wheels, and several hard chairs.

The Business Model

Members of helping professions are accustomed to providing services within the context of a value system. Sometimes our values are explicit and codified; more often they are unstated. Seldom, however, are they questioned publicly, and that is precisely what we intend to do now.

All professionals share a body of knowledge and a code of ethics. Nothing in the recommendation that ensues should be interpreted to connote that we favor counseling services stemming from ignorance rather than fact, or that we propose unethical treatment of clients. We do question, however, the widely accepted idea that the profession should maintain an attitude of aloof distance from clients and should *never* advertise the availability of ameliorative or remedial services. It has been demonstrated factually and is beyond dispute that the SSS are not referring themselves for counseling services that might minimize some of their distress. As an alternative to the traditional "professional" stance of not advertising and waiting for clientele to refer themselves, we propose an aggressive business model of advertising, designed specifically to inform a potential clientele of available services. To be more specific, we advocate the use of advertising media to disseminate relevant information: any combination of bilingual announcements on television programs or radio stations that cater to the SSS; ads in Spanish- and English-language newspapers; posters at community gathering places or at events that will attract people; and finally, informational programs at educational institutions.

Some readers may be offended by a recommendation perceived as a breach of traditional professional ethics. We can only point out that the recommendation makes the most sense for community agencies; few professionals in private practice would find it commercially feasible to launch an advertising campaign to attract an impoverished clientele. Furthermore, this is exactly the model adopted by the U.S. health professions to draw attention to other serious social problems. Reflect, for example, upon the well-advertised campaigns to eliminate drunken driving, to lessen the use of addictive drugs, or to warn teenagers of the danger signs of venereal disease. Consider further how the public is bombarded with information about the incidence of lung cancer among smokers. And finally, consider the enormous publicity promoting examinations for breast cancer following the illness and surgery of the wife of the President of the United States.

Community Involvement

The significance of this recommendation cannot be overestimated; it is crucial to the successful operation of any program designed to motivate more of the SSS to seek counseling. The basic issue is that the target population must sincerely believe that the agency offers relevant services, operates in their best interests, and is really theirs. The criterion of relevance is best met by assessing the counseling needs of the local population, and on the basis of preconceived notions appropriate for similar groups. Such services are discussed below in the sections on "Traditional Counseling Methods With the SSS" and "Cultural Innovations."

To convince a clientele that a given agency operates in their best interests requires, at a minimum, that the appropriate services be *offered*. Second, the "good news" must be broadly and rapidly disseminated among the potential client population by using the socially acceptable techniques of propaganda and public relations. It makes good sense to post announcements printed in two languages in neighborhoods where the potential clientele is heavily SSS. In the centers themselves, of course, directional signs should be bilingual.

A third recommendation is to employ community relations and ethnically similar personnel at administrative, professional, and para-professional levels, and to appoint these persons (without pay where appropriate) to policy-making positions where they can contribute to major decisions concerning the counseling services. This includes governing bodies or boards of directors who set general policy, as well as specific committees that make day-to-day decisions, such as whether a given research project or service program may be launched or supported. We believe that community people will be convinced that a counseling service delivery agency is really theirs only when they possess the power to make these kinds of decisions.

We recommend that community mental health centers and other counseling facilities located in areas with a high proportion of SSS should organize "alumni" groups of exclients. Groups such as "Friends of the Center" could be organized from community residents. One major objective of these groups would be to recommend the center to community residents and to encourage use of its services. This procedure may be viewed as a creative use of cultural values because it responds to the SSS's need for a more personal matching of services to potential clients. Personal sponsorship could be developed through bimonthly orientation meetings at which the friends and alumni would be brought up to date on new developments by the center's staff. Friends and alumni could recommend staff members by name to community residents who need help. The potential client would be less inhibited and more likely to approach the center if he knew he was coming to meet a specific person by referral from an acquaintance, rather than becoming another faceless number in the center's computer.

Our final recommendation for making community residents believe that the agency is really theirs is to encourage the use of agency facilities for community activities. Organized groups within the community could be permitted, or even encouraged, to use agency facilities for meetings. Where such groups do not exist, the agency could help create them. The agency could combine open house operations with festive activities on holidays important to the bicultural population, that is, not just on the Fourth of July or Memorial Day, but also on *Cinco de Mayo* and *el 16 de Septiembre*. It is our belief—based on our knowledge of

Latino culture and demography, rather than on any experimentally based data—that modifications of this kind will motivate greater numbers of self-referrals.

Training Programs

We assume that most counselors maintain professional standards by constantly striving to improve the quality of their skills. They usually accomplish this informally by keeping up on the literature, by consulting by telephone and in person with colleagues, and of course by remaining active in counseling relationships. Some agencies offer seminars, workshops, lecture series, and consultant visits as a more formal means of facilitating this process; and some counselors take advantage of these educational opportunities. We support wholeheartedly the continuation of such approaches, but ask only that such programs be tailored to the specific needs of the Spanish-speaking population.

The first point is that the SSS population has a somewhat different pattern of social and personal problems and a vastly different response to standard counseling methods. Thus counselors should have special training to deal with the high frequency problems which afflict the SSS as a result of high unemployment combined with low educational achievement. Unskilled workers with minimal education will find it difficult to find employment.

The second relevant point is that SSS are vastly underrepresented in disciplines which deliver counseling services or which conduct the necessary research. Thus the prevailing situation is that the SSS require special counseling methods related to their culture-specific value systems; yet few professionals are skilled in counseling and are also knowledgeable about the SSS culture groups. The ideal and ultimate solution is to educate the SSS in both service and research counseling. Even a crash program to create SSS professional counselors, however, would require at least a decade from the point of inception to the point at which the SSS would be able to receive culturally relevant counseling. Elsewhere we documented our opinion that it appears unlikely that much significant change will occur in the foreseeable future (Padilla, Ruiz, & Alvarez, 1975). It seems much more likely that the SSS population will continue to receive counseling services from (1) traditionally educated Anglo professionals whose knowledge of SSS culture (if any) comes from training programs, or (2) SSS para-professionals whose knowledge of counseling comes from subdoctoral training programs.

Relevant training programs must be created for specific needs. We have already advocated the employment of community residents as para-professionals, and it appears that these people could form a training cadre to educate non-Latino counselors. There are a variety of educational approaches for teaching counseling skills to SSS para-professionals. These include one-to-one supervision, group supervision using audio- or videotapes, bibliographic references, group discussions and seminars, and formal lectures and workshops. Both professionals and para-professionals can simultaneously acquire skills from each other when matched pairs function as therapist and co-therapist in the actual operation of a counseling group. Ruiz and Burgess (1968) discuss how these and other methods can be used to teach such skills.

Traditional Counseling Methods With the SSS

Traditional counseling methods have proven relatively ineffectual with SSS clients. It is extremely difficult to explain why this is so, but any one or more of the following reasons may provide a partial explanation:

1. Measurement problems in outcome research on psychotherapy are not yet unresolved, and thus

there are no agreed upon criteria to denote "success."

2. Counseling is, in general, equally ineffectual with the lower socioeconomic status (SES) groups. Because a high proportion of SSS are low SES, the problem of explaining therapeutic failure is compounded.

3. Many behaviors manifested by the SSS (and the poor) in response to counseling can be construed as indices of counseling failure or as reasons for failure by those who do not tailor therapeutic programs to fit the needs of different culture groups. These indices include such behavior as failure to keep appointments, premature termination, or failure to follow advice.

4. Inadequate attention is paid to cultural and subcultural differences.

Despite these conceptual and measurement difficulties, and even in the absence of research showing that counseling really works, we recommend that effort be expended to modify traditional methods so that they become more culturally relevant. For example, attitudes toward time seem to vary across cultures (Stone & Ruiz, 1974). Thus counseling might become more effective if the concept of the 50-minute hour were de-emphasized, if greater latitude were exercised in beginning or ending the session promptly, and if maximum attention were devoted to process and outcome. After all, the ultimate goal of counseling is constructive behavior change; the temporal context in which this occurs is only secondary.

As a second example, patterns of social interaction vary across cultures and the SSS will be particularly sensitive to social behavior. Thus the counselor is advised to shake hands, or even to embrace clients occasionally, because the SSS emphasize physical contact in social relations. So-called small talk might be permitted or even encouraged with SSS clients more than with non-SSS clients. Social chitchat is not necessarily defensive; rather it seems to reflect the greater value the SSS place upon casual social interaction. At the risk of promulgating gross overgeneralizations with potentially racist overtones, many of the SSS appear more extraversive, or people-oriented, than many members of other cultures. Go to a Latino wedding, a baptismal party, or a fiesta and you will observe people standing close together, often touching, and conversing in animated tones. The sensitive counselor will try to incorporate these observations into counseling procedures and practices.

It is essential to keep in mind other culturally and demographically unique aspects of the client group. Among the SSS, families are larger, younger, and appear more cohesive than among other groups; thus the incidence of divorce, separation, or single-parent families is lower. The family assumes greater importance in the day-to-day life and overall general adjustment of SSS clients. The extended family system is typical; and, as expected, sex roles are more rigidly defined, greater respect is shown for the aged, and fathers typically enjoy greater authority and/or prestige. These factors suggest the general recommendation that family approaches be used more often—for example, in cases where individual counseling is more typical for specific problems such as drug or alcohol abuse, criminal recidivism, and so forth. Group approaches would probably be less efficient in other cases, such as vocational or academic counseling.

In family counseling it makes sense for the counselor to listen respectfully to opinions voiced by SSS fathers and elders, thus emulating the behavior of other family members. While elders are speaking, the silence of the young, and their tendency to respond rather than initiate conversation, may be interpreted as respect for the wisdom of age.

We are not deluded into assuming that Latino young are paragons of virtue. Silence will occasionally denote distraction or low interest, as it does among other clients. If the counselor needs to validate this hypothesis, he may attend to body language and refocus the attention of the young by asking questions such as, "How would you summarize what your Papa just said?" Deference toward males does not mean that mothers and other females are mute or without influence within SSS families. Rather their contributions to decision making are more subtle. If the non-Latino counselor attends carefully, he will observe how SSS parents cooperate in decision making; the skilled counselor will employ these cultural styles for therapeutic benefit.

Counselors in general, and non-Latino counselors in particular, may experience difficulty dealing with certain aspects of intergenerational relations within the SSS family. Children typically retain close ties with parents and the extended family even after marriage. Counselors unfamiliar with this cultural attribute may misinterpret such behavior as immature dependence (a "liability"), rather than as adaptive re-affirmation of a source of current and future emotional support. We suspect that this is so, but we lack experimental or empirical documentation for our conclusion. The historical cohesion of the extended family is breaking down as the SSS young become more familiar with the newer American ways.

Another source of conflict and one rarely mentioned in social science literature is that younger, more assertive "Chicanos," insisting upon rights of citizenship, often disagree with older, less assertive "Mexican Americans," who sometimes complain that the young are excessively aggressive (Alvarez, 1974). This discrepancy between labels, and the correlated behavioral differences, illustrate once again the critical significance of accurately assessing ethnic identification, even within the same ethnic group.

Counselors should be alert to the fact that many of

their SSS clients will prefer and seek a counseling relationship in which they are given advice and instructions to resolve specific problems. Their analogue will be the medical model in which the patient presents a problem, then assumes a passive role as the doctor prescribes medication or some other form of organic treatment. Thus, when the SSS client is requested to provide a review of childhood experiences, or when the counseling interview is structured so that the client is expected to reflect introspectively, the SSS client may be confused. This observation does not imply that the SSS are passive-dependent or incapable of introspection, but rather that the customary nondirective counseling interview may violate their expectations. Thus the sophisticated counselor will be more active with the SSS client, both by explaining why seemingly irrelevant information may help resolve a given problem, and by providing advice and instructions when such intervention seems appropriate.

Counseling Innovations

This concluding section presents recommendations for the counseling of SSS clients that are innovative in several senses. These recommendations have seldom been tried before, perhaps because they do not flow smoothly from traditional or common counseling practice. Some recommendations concern both theory and method. For example, earlier we suggested that the culture of SSS clients is such that approaches drawing on the unity and strengths of the extended family system should be applied with greater frequency. Other recommendations are programmatic. We urge that counseling agencies relax their institutional rigidity by altering schedules, changing priorities, and introducing new counseling programs to deal with some of the problems of the poor and of ethnic minority group clients that have been largely ignored up to now. Finally, we present these recommendations despite the fact that there is no body of empirical evidence to validate their application in any rigorous psychometric sense. Nevertheless, we feel justified in proposing these recommendations, not only because they offer potential solutions to social problems of significant severity, but also because older methods have failed. Our intention is to set in motion the process of creating innovative counseling methods for the SSS client.

The next two recommendations form a theme which will characterize the spirit of the remainder of this chapter. First, we strongly urge a program to assess needs before the systematic delivery of any counseling services to any SSS neighborhood. Residents of the SSS community, as well as SSS professionals and para-professionals, must share in the planning and execution of this assessment of needs. Otherwise measurements may be culturally irrelevant or inaccurate and may result in the creation of counseling programs that are inefficient and irrelevant. The suggestion that community residents participate in research dovetails perfectly with our earlier recommendation for training programs in research skills for para-professional staff (see "Training Programs").

The second thematic suggestion has already appeared in various sections of the preceding discussion. Here we expand upon the idea that people will be more likely to refer themselves for counseling when a center offers services that have been revealed by a valid, community-generated assessment of needs.

Let us assume, for example, that a needs assessment indicates abuse of addictive drugs among the young. All the resources and potential treatment methods we have discussed up to this point can be applied. We suggested earlier (see "Business Model") that a multimedia advertising campaign be initiated to disseminate information about available programs. Culture-specific treatment programs with drug users and addicts can be launched using community residents as para-professional counselors. If more culture-specific information of an empirical nature seems necessary, then relevant data can be generated by social scientists working in collaboration with community residents trained as researchers (see "Training Programs").

One possible finding might be that experimentation with drugs begins at a relatively young age. In such a case counselors could create and deliver informational and drug abuse prevention programs, possibly coordinating these programs with curricula involving primary and elementary students and with school activities involving teachers and parents. A second possible research finding might be that drug abuse and addiction can be minimized by using an approach that exploits the strengths of the extended family. Such a finding would obviously support the expansion of family counseling services for potential and identified drug users. The model being proposed involves the identification of a specific problem among a specific sample (drug addiction among the young); the creation and dissemination of the appropriate information to the target population (i.e., "Drugs are bad," and "If you are hooked we can help you,"); the application of culture specific-treatment methods (e.g., family-oriented group treatment); and finally, an ongoing research program to determine whether the target population is being contacted and if the treatment methods are successful.

This hypothetical instance of drug abuse among the young is common to a variety of cultures and communities. Furthermore, results of treatment approaches have been disappointing because recidivism is high and success rates are low. Let us therefore apply the model to some social problems which are somewhat more characteristic of the SSS and which may prove more responsive to therapeutic intervention.

One major problem of the SSS is related to academic-vocational behaviors. We know that SSS students are older than other pupils in their grade, perform poorly on tests of general intelligence and academic achievement (and subsequently are over-represented in special education classes), are more frequently counseled into vocational rather than academic curricula, and terminate their education at an earlier level than the general population. As noted before, SSS adults subsequently work in occupations that require little education, have minimal opportunities for vocational advancement, and have high unemployment rates, especially during economic recessions. Any agency offering counseling services has the potential to offer youngsters relevant information (e.g., available scholarships), and to provide them with the incentive necessary to remain in school and to advance themselves through education. It seems feasible to create counseling programs which combine, for example, participation in athletic activities at the counseling agency with periodic visits from renowned sports personalities who can encourage achievement through education. Young SSS clients could be encouraged to participate in educational programs dealing with psychological tests so that familiarity through exposure will come to equal that observed in middle-class individuals. If necessary, remedial education and tutorial programs can be integrated with more traditional counseling services. Agencies can be modified to provide counseling that lessens some of the social stresses experienced by the SSS when they are misclassified by test scores achieved on culturally biased measures.

Continuing in the spirit of recommending programs designed to maintain personality integration by minimizing social stress, we advocate intervention in client employability. Some adult clients could be encouraged to return to school. Advice to pursue a given course of study should, of course, be integrated with the client's skills and the dissemination of accurate information concerning the probability of employment and opportunity in that particular field. Ancillary programs designed to help job applicants become more attractive to potential employers are highly useful, for example, teaching barrio youth how to complete application forms and how to conduct themselves during job interviews.

Counseling techniques and agencies can do much to make the declining years of the SSS elderly more comfortable. Imagine the intensity of their distress. First, they experience all the problems of the old—declining health, decreased vigor, restricted mobility, loneliness, and boredom. Second, they experience all the problems of the poor —incomes remaining low and fixed in an inflationary economy, resulting in a declining standard of living. Finally, many SSS elderly are monolingual or dominant in Spanish, less acculturated than younger SSS, and therefore removed even further from sources of community support available to the non-SSS elderly.

To be maximally helpful with this group, counseling services can be extended to cover both physical and psychological needs. Agencies can monitor dental and medical problems, can make sure that living conditions are healthy, and can help maintain nutrition by providing a daily hot meal. The mealtime can be combined with informal counseling sessions designed to help people get to know each other better, share successful problem-solving mechanisms, interact, and combat loneliness. In addition, the elderly could be offered age-specific opportunities for recreation, entertainment, and education.

Our final recommendation concerns the establishment of a culturally relevant crisis intervention service, possibly including 24-hour phone service by bilingual operators. Problems that appear trivial and are dealt with easily in middle-class settings frequently loom as major crises to the monolingual SSS poor or to highly marginal individuals. An approaching winter combined with a landlord who charges exorbitant rents but refuses to repair broken windows can throw an SSS welfare mother into a panic of perceived powerlessness. An unemployed SSS widow with poor English fluency can be catapulted into a life-threatening crisis by harassment from monolingual English creditors if at the same time the landlord threatens eviction and the police arrest her son for reasons she does not understand. Problems of this complexity and severity are unfortunately much too common among the SSS poor.

Note immediately that traditional theories of counseling do not readily accommodate real life problems such as those described above. As a result, counselors and agencies may be slow to react because appropriate therapeutic responses do not come to mind easily. These particular clients do not need insight, psychodynamic exploration, or enhanced self-actualization. Supportive responses might minimize their immediate distress somewhat, but their basic problems remain untouched. They need bona fide crisis intervention: someone to contact the police for further information, to arrange legal consultation, to obtain emergency funding, to expedite a delayed check, to intercede with impatient creditors. If and when individual counselors and service agencies develop the flexibility needed to provide these kinds of services, we may be taking the first steps toward the resolution of major problems among the SSS.

REFERENCES

Abad, V., Ramos, J., & Boyce, E. A model for delivery of mental services to Spanish-speaking minorities. *American Journal of Orthopsychiatry,* 1974, *44,* 584–595.

Acosta, F. X. Mexican American and Anglo American reactions to ethnically similar and dissimilar psychotherapists. in R. Alvarez (Ed.), *Delivery of services for latino community mental health.* Monograph Number Two, SSMHR & D. Program, University of California, Los Angeles, 1975, pp. 51–80.

Alvarez, R., et al. *Latino community mental health.* Monograph Number One, SSMHR & D Program, University of California, Los Angeles, 1974.

Bachrach, L. L. Utilization of State and County mental hospitals by Spanish Americans in 1972, Statistical Note 116, 1975, DHEW Publication No. (ADM) 75–158.

Bloombaum, M., Yamamoto, J., & Evans, Q. Cultural stereotyping among psychotherapists. *Journal of Counseling and Clinical Psychology,* 1968, *32,* 99.

Cobb, C. W. Community mental health services and the lower socioeconomic class: A summary of research literature on outpatient treatment (1963–1969). *American Journal of Orthopsychiatry,* 1972, *42,* 401–414.

Edgerton, R. B., Karno, M., & Fernandez, I. Curanderismo in the metropolis: The diminishing rule of folk-psychiatry among Los Angeles Mexican Americans. *American Journal of Psychotherapy,* 1970, *24,* 124–134.

Edgerton, R. B. & Karno, M. Mexican-American bilingualism and the perception of mental illness. *Archives of General Psychiatry,* 1971, *24,* 286–290.

Gordon, S. Are we seeing the right patients? Child guidance intake: the sacred cow. *American Journal of Orthopsychiatry,* 1965, *35,* 131–137.

Jaco, E. G. *The social epidemiology of mental disorders: A psychiatric survey of Texas.* New York: Russell Sage Foundation, 1960.

Karno, M., & Edgerton, R. B. Perception of mental illness in a Mexican American community. *Archives of General Psychiatry,* 1969, *20,* 233–238.

Kline, L. Y. Some factors in the psychiatric treatment of Spanish Americans. *American Journal of Psychiatry,* 1969, *125,* 1674–1681.

Lorion, R. P. Patient and therapist variables in the treatment of low-income patients. *Psychological Bulletin,* 1974, *81,* 344–354.

Lorion, R. P. Socioeconomic status and traditional treatment approaches reconsidered. *Psychological Bulletin,* 1973, *79,* 263–270.

Padilla, A. M., & Ruiz, R. A. *Latino mental health: A review of literature.* Washington, D.C.: U.S. Government Printing Office, 1973.

Padilla, A. M., Ruiz, R. A., & Alvarez, R. Community mental health services for the Spanish-speaking/surnamed population. *American Psychologist,* 1975, *30,* 892–905.

Perez, M. S. Counseling services at UCSC: Attitudes and perspectives of Chicano students. Unpublished manuscript, 1975.

Phillipus, M. J. Successful and unsuccessful approaches to mental health services for an urban Hispano-American population. *Journal of Public Health,* 1971, *61,* 820–830.

Ruiz, R. A. Relative frequency of Americans with Spanish surnames in associations of psychology, psychiatry, and sociology. *American Psychologist,* 1971, *26,* 1022–1024.

Ruiz, R. A., & Burgess, M. M. Group psychotherapy: A preliminary teaching model. *Journal of Medical Education,* 1968, *43,* 455–463.

Ruiz, R. A., & Wrenn, R. L. *The Healthy Personality,* Monterrey, California: Brooks-Cole, in press.

Stone, P. C., & Ruiz, R. A. Race and class as differential determinants of underachievement and underaspiration among Mexican Americans. *Journal of Educational Research,* 1974, *68,* 51–56.

Stonequist, F. U. *The marginal man: A study in personality and culture conflict.* New York: Russell and Russell, Inc., 1937.

Torrey, E. F. *The mind game: Witchdoctors and psychiatrists.* New York: Emerson Hall, 1972.

Wolkon, G. H., Miriwaki, S., Mandel, D. M., Archuleta, D. Jr., Bunje, P. & Zimmerman, S. Ethnicity and social class in the delivery of services: Analysis of a child guidance clinic. *American Journal of Public Health,* 1974, *64,* 709–712.

Wrenn, R. L., & Ruiz, R. A. *The normal personality: Issues to insight.* Monterrey, California: Brooks-Cole, 1970.

Yamamoto, J., James, Q. C., & Palley, N. Cultural problems in psychiatric therapy. *Archives of General Psychiatry,* 1968, *19,* 45–49.

Chapter 2

COUNSELING ALASKAN NATIVES

Bill Richards
Charles Oxereok

This chapter describes some of the unique social and cultural factors currently influencing the work of counselors in Alaska. These include new developments in transportation, communications, economics, population growth, political organization, and in the delivery system for mental health services. To make relevant interventions in this unique setting, counselors are having to develop new roles and techniques. Some examples from clinical practice are presented that illustrate the kinds of counseling problems that might be encountered, followed by a discussion of the implications for counselors.

Alaska is unique today because of the pace, scope, and complexity of the social and cultural changes it is experiencing. These changes are leading to new types of counseling problems for Alaska Natives that are not easily classified or studied, and to new types of counseling roles and strategies. Sociocultural change is, of course, not the sole explanation for behavior. One has to consider physiological and biological factors, psychological factors, situational factors, and historical factors, among others, in trying to understand why persons act as they do. Moreover, no one really knows very much about the impact of sociocultural factors on behavior. The fields of social and cross-cultural psychology are still in early stages of development. This socio-cultural dimension of behavior, however, is the key to any discussion of counseling methods appropriate for Alaska Natives.

SOCIOCULTURAL FORCES AT WORK IN ALASKA IN 1975

Diverse Eco-Systems

Until very recently, many places in Alaska were extremely isolated because of the harsh climate, long distances involved in traveling from place to place, lack of roads, rough terrain, and infrequent or nonexistent air travel. In addition, the major groups of Eskimos, Athabascans, Aleuts, Tlingit-Haida, and Shimsham have had widely varying regional and local customs. The state therefore consisted of a number of ecological systems that until recently operated relatively independently.

Transportation and Communication Developments

Rapid developments in transportation and communications in Alaska are causing abrupt and significant change. For example, in 1966 a mental health consultant would spend nearly 6 hours flying from Anchorage to Bethel. This trip now takes only an hour. Some parts of the state—Anchorage, Fairbanks, Fort Yukon—now have the capability of *instant* visual and audio communication through a communications satellite (Wilson & Brady, 1975). It will not be long before almost every village in Alaska has TV reception. (There are now 15 native communities with satellite TV reception.) These developments mean that parts of the state that before were relatively inaccessible and "bush" will become increasingly suburban in character.

With these changes will come major shifts in nearly

every aspect of village life. Village people that before would have had little exposure to nonnative mental health concepts or access to professional counselors will soon be watching this season's TV doctors counseling their patients, and will be only a short air hop from professional help.

Pipeline Boom

Another major development has been the pipeline boom, which has been bringing tremendous economic development to the state. The pipeline's impact, like that of the transportation and communication developments, is difficult to quantitate but seems to be having far-reaching effects. These effects both resolve and create counseling problems. For example, men formerly depressed because they were unemployed may have emerged from that depression because they now hold high-paying jobs. Others who were formerly well adjusted may now be facing a major disruption in their lives because their former hunting land may have been taken over by the state as oil property.

Our suspicion is that many of the changes taking place in Alaska will prove ultimately to have been connected directly or indirectly to the impact of the pipeline. The discovery of massive oil reserves in locations where title to the land was unclear undoubtedly influenced decisions both about Alaska's becoming a state in the fifties and about the Land Claims Settlement with Alaska Natives in 1971. As "the world's largest private construction effort" (*Time Magazine,* June 1975) goes into effect, tremendous financial inducements are being offered to groups within the state that are changing their customary way of operating. For example, Alaska Natives are told they can receive large sums of land claims money, provided that they organize into corporate structures to manage the funds. A "corporate culture" is thus being imposed on the diverse cultural groups in the state, and no native is unaffected. Besides hunting and fishing, natives now need to know about such things as proxy votes, stockholders' meetings, and oil lease arrangements. All sorts of psychological stresses are created by the conflict between traditional ways and the ways of "sophisticated money," and counselors in Alaska will have to contend with these stresses more and more.

Population Changes

Associated with the pipeline boom is a very rapid population growth (*Alaska Review of Business and Economic Conditions*, March 1972; *Alaska Natives and the Land*, 1968). For example, Alaska's population in 1973 was about 300,000. In 1974 the figure had risen to 324,000, and it was projected that by the end of 1975 the figure would be close to 475,000. Of this total, roughly 85,000 people are Alaska Natives. Compared to the 1940s, when the Alaska Native population accounted for nearly half of the total state population, the environment faced by today's counselors has obviously changed considerably.

Alaska is also experiencing an influx of psychiatrists and other mental health professionals. In the 1950s and early 1960s, only one or two private psychiatrists were practicing in the whole state. In 1975 there were 14 private psychiatrists, and 16 psychiatrists in public programs run by the public health service, state, and military. Close to 40% of the total psychiatric manpower in the state has arrived within the past two years. Mental health problems that were not even addressed in the past may soon be receiving attention as a result of this influx of professional manpower.

In the past many of the psychiatrists concentrated on working in the largest city, Anchorage, and Alaska Natives in villages were virtually ignored. This situation has now begun to change, and it could change even more depending on what form of national health insurance is eventually adopted. Alaska Natives who now have to utilize public programs for counseling may soon have the option of consulting private practitioners or professionals under contract to their native organizations.

Legislation and Political Reorganizations

Two very important recent legislative decisions are also affecting health delivery for Alaska Natives. First, the Alaska Native Land Claims Settlement Act of 1971 (Alaska Native Claims Settlement Act: House of Representative Report No. 92–746, December 1971) has resulted in the formation of 12 Native Regional Corporations in the state (see Figure 2–1). Each of these corporations has two major divisions—one is a profit-making division to manage land investments, etc., and the other is a nonprofit wing to develop health, education, and social services for the residents of the region (see Figure 2–2). These nonprofit wings are forming regional health organizations that are very actively committed to developing rural health programs, and that have access to substantial financial resources to do so.

The second major legislative enactment that promises to have a major impact is the Self-Determination Act of 1976 (Public Law 93–638 93rd Congress, S. 1017, January 4, 1975). This act provides for contracting with Indian Health Service and BIA programs for services to tribal groups, and detailing personnel from these agencies to work directly under native leadership. The goal of this legislation is to make it possible for Indian and Alaska Native groups to take over direction of their own health programs. Because of the organizational developments spurred by the Land Claims Settlement Act, Regional Native Health Organizations are in an excellent position to take full advantage of this new law.

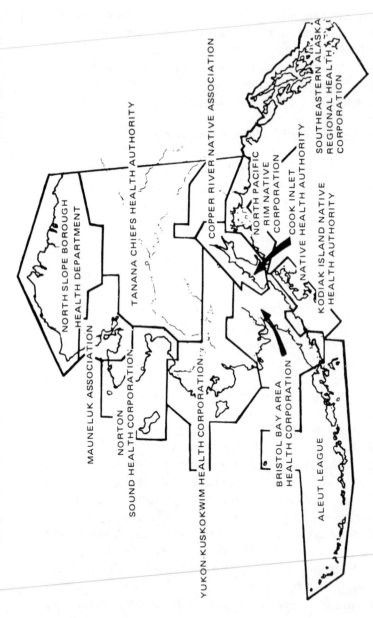

Fig. 2-1. Counseling in Alaska is being very much affected by political, economic, and organizational changes resulting from the Alaska Native Claims Settlement Act and Self-Determination Act. The attached map shows regional corporations established under the Claims Act.

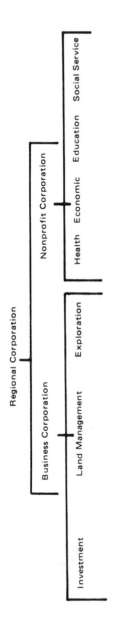

Regional Corporation

Business Corporation

Investment · Land Management · Exploration

Nonprofit Corporation

Health · Economic · Education · Social Service

Post Land Claims Settlement Act: Regional Corporation Structure

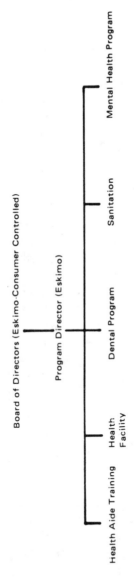

Board of Directors (Eskimo-Consumer Controlled)

Program Director (Eskimo)

Health Aide Training · Health Facility · Dental Program · Sanitation · Mental Health Program

Health Corporation Structure (Model-Yukon-Kuskokwim Health Corporation—Bethel, Alaska)

Fig. 2–2. This diagram shows the profit-making and nonprofit-making structure of a typical corporation.

Changes in the Mental Health Delivery System

It is probably as difficult for counselors to appreciate these transportation, communication, and organizational break-throughs as it was for blacksmiths to appreciate the invention of the horseless carriage. It can be rather unnerving when, during a tele-medicine consultation with Fort Yukon, one finds oneself nodding one's head and saying "uh-huh" to a TV set. Videophone and computerized information capabilities will probably radically change our mental health counseling operations in the state within the next few years. Counselors of the future are going to need a bewildering range of skills, including knowledge about such things as computers, telecommunications, and corporate law, but most of all about cultural lifestyle of the vanishing native people of Alaska.

To expand a little on the significance of these changes for counselors, we need to examine a bit of history. In the past mental health services to Alaska Natives were delivered mainly by government programs. Alaska was a territory until 1959 and this meant that many federal programs were developed to deliver services in the state. When Alaska became a state in 1959, many state agency programs were quickly developed (Schrader, 1973). The tax base was inadequate to fund the state programs, because oil revenues have not yet started to come in. Alaska was left with a very poorly planned nonsystem of federal and state programs, with overlapping jurisdictions, poorly defined responsibilities, and large areas of coverage.

Attempts to unravel these overlapping, confusing responsibilities are compounded because of transportation and communication problems in the state. At the present time an individual patient or client might be obtaining public health nursing from one region, medical care from another, and alcohol counseling from still another. Counselors experience difficulty in trying to work out coordinated services for patients, or followup activities for patients who may be counseled briefly in the city and then return to an isolated village thousands of miles away. It is not uncommon to see patients who are trying to contend with 10 or 11 agencies at once, and counselors who have been trained in "one-to-one insight-oriented counseling" may experience great difficulties in dealing with all of these various competing groups. One of the most common counseling problems is the patient with too many counselors, all working in an uncoordinated fashion on different parts of the patient's problem, and often giving conflicting information or advice. Attempts are now being made to get all of the state, federal, and municipal programs to use the regional health boundaries as established by the Native Claims Settlement Act.

IMPLICATIONS FOR COUNSELORS

The examples below illustrate in some detail the sort of clinical problems a counselor can expect to encounter among Alaska Natives. These case reports are a discussion of new counseling roles and techniques that are evolving to respond to these problems.

Case 1

Frances is a 13-year-old Eskimo in the seventh grade. She was put up for adoption at an early age, then transferred from one foster family to another. By age 13, she had had many sets of foster parents and several counselors and social workers, and she was considered a behavior problem in school.

Because her community did not have a school, she was sent several thousand miles away from her current foster family to attend a boarding school. Communications difficulties prevented us from communicating immediately with her foster family or her current social worker to get information that might help us understand her counseling needs better. Hospital records and school records from her previous schools were also not immediately available because of these same transportation and communication problems. In addition, political reorganization in the area where the girl was currently going to school had just transferred the school from management by the state to management by a local native corporation.

Because the native group had not had previous experience with managing boarding schools, procedures were not well organized for providing counseling to students, and many of the staff were unclear about who was supposed to do what. The nearest professional counseling resources were also several hundred miles away from the school. Because of overlapping responsibilities, it was unclear whether the State Mental Health Clinic, a federal mental health program, or school counselors from another school should see the girl. Here is what Frances had to say about how she saw her life and her current problems:

> I was born in a town and I was put in a foster home when I was just a child. I lived with them for about 6 years and the welfare took me away from them and put me in another foster home. I lived with her in one town for a year and we moved to another town and lived with her for another 2 years. Then welfare took me away from her because I was getting a little too bouncy for her 'cause she was getting old. Then when welfare took me away from her, a welfare officer drove me down to a big city and brought me down to the children's home, and I stayed there until I was ready to go to another foster home. Then they started to let me visit a home every weekend, and after a while I moved in with them and I lived with them for 1 year and 3 months because they got a divorce and I didn't want to live with them. Then I was put back in the children's home, and after a while I was put in with another couple for about 8 or 9 months and didn't

like it because I didn't like the way he handled the family. I can't explain it. I was put back in the children's home again. Before I moved in with this family I was put in another foster home and I was forced to leave them because he was a state trooper and the state said he was transferred to a village and I couldn't go there because there wasn't a welfare office and if any welfare officer wanted to see me he'd have to drive all the way down to see me. Then I was put in another foster home. And that's the story of my life.

Frances considered that she had no individual problems and that she was coping as best she could with a "sick" social and school system. She thought that the school teacher who was concerned about her school behavior—truancy, not paying attention in class—was crazy himself.

How would you, as a counselor, try to help Frances? This sort of situation is not uncommon, and there are obviously no easy answers.

Case 2

Peter is a 21-year-old Tlingit boy in the twelfth grade. Like Frances, he was attending a boarding school far away from his home and family. Although this school was better managed than the one described above, classes were large, no native teachers were on the staff, and no special counseling arrangements were available for students. The federal and state agencies in the area had unclear, overlapping responsibilities, and each assumed that the other was providing counseling services to the school. The boy was in classes with students from quite different backgrounds, with widely varying interests and abilities. Some were upper middle-class white students who had lived all their lives in a big city and spoke English fluently. Others, like himself, came from small villages many miles away, and experienced confusion and anxiety trying to adjust to city life and to speaking English.

The young man was highly respected in his village because he was a good hunter and fisherman. He was considered a failure and a counseling problem by his teachers, however, because he did not appear to be interested in school subjects, never did his homework, and spent most of his time in class seeming to daydream, doodling pictures about fishing and hunting back home. He got into fights with other students who teased him about being slow.

Here is what Peter had to say about how he viewed his current situation:

> Well, to make a long story short, I'll start how we lived different from different people of Alaska. All people put up food for the winter, or let me put it this way. They start in the springtime like we pick seaweed, put them out in the sun to dry, then put the seaweed in bags or can. Then the big hunt in the spring is seal. We go hunting for maybe 4–5 days and troll same time for king salmon. Maybe we would get really lucky for the hunting and trolling. We skin all the seals. Give all the seal meat away to all the people that live in the village or most of the seal meat to the old timers that can't go hunting or sick. The fish that we catch we sell to the cold storage. Maybe make about a couple hundred bucks a trip. The summer coming up we make fishing in the summer we go seining for the fishing company. I think we got the biggest fishing fleet in southeast Alaska. Hunting, trolling all in the fall because everything open then. Winter comes—then we eat all the food we put up. Go hunting for deer until season is closed December 31. Do all sorts of things like sports in winter. Well, nothing really to talk about our way of living, but been proud Indian!

How would you approach this situation? Here again, there is no easy answer. It is probably realistic to view the boy's school behavior as a normal adaptation by a "proud Indian" to a system that is not responding to his needs or a conflict between cultural values, rather than as a "counseling problem." The fact remains, however, that if you begin to "counsel" Alaska Natives, you will soon run into

many very similar situations labeled "counseling problems." Many cases do not fall into well-accepted syn-
dromes. Data collected on mental health problems may
also not fully document complex situations such as those
described above. This makes it difficult to outline systematic counseling methods for Alaska Natives, because what
is meant by a "counseling problem" is often unclear.

SOME APPROACHES TO COUNSELING IN THE UNIQUE ALASKA ENVIRONMENT

It would be unusual to encounter any two counselors who
view what they are doing in exactly the same way or who
respond to complexities within the counseling environment with exactly the same techniques, but it is even more
rare in Alaska. What follow, then, are descriptions of various approaches to the unique social and culture factors in
Alaska with which counselors have to deal.

Circumventing Transportation and Communication Problems

THE FLYING COUNSELOR.   To circumvent transportation
problems, some counselors take flying lessons and buy
their own planes. Others fly on commercial aircraft, alone
or in multidisciplinary teams, thousands of miles each year.
Still others are experimenting with counseling by telephone, video, or by mail, but these efforts always seem less
effective than face-to-face communication.

DECENTRALIZED SERVICES.   Another approach to the problem of decreasing distances between people and counseling resources is the development of local mental health
teams. A variety of storefront operations, staffed by native

counselors who live in the region, has now been established in many parts of the state (Bloom & Richards, 1974; Coleman et al., 1974; Feigin, 1974; Kraus, 1976; Stillner, 1974). Overall direction for these programs is typically provided by a board of older, experienced native leaders. A Native person manages the mental health team. One or more non-native professionals may be on the staff to serve as trainers or backup for native counselors in the villages. Screening, early detection of counseling problems, brief counseling, or followup treatments can be carried out at the village level with this sort of system. More sophisticated diagnostic procedures can be conducted by the backup professionals, as well as more intensive treatment. Some patients will still have to fly many miles under this system if they need very specialized evaluation and treatment that can be provided only in Anchorage, or if they need hospitalization. But most patients can be treated close to their homes.

COMMUNICATIONS.   As far as communication strategies are concerned, the range of responses varies from cussing the telephone after the thirty-fifth try to get through, to working with groups trying to establish telecommunications satellite projects in the state. By 1980 many situations now handled by a time-consuming airplane flight may be solved by an instantaneous satellite videophone call. Some counselors are planning on getting specialized training in communications technology, computerized data systems, and telemedicine, so that they will be able to be knowledgeable about and take advantage of these developments.

TRAINING FOR WORK IN ISOLATED AREAS.   Some counselors, realizing that they may be working in places with limited resources and that they may need additional skills, try to get additional training as generalists. For example, a psychiatrist planning to practice in the "bush" (the Alaskan term for remote areas) may take refresher courses in general medicine, knowing that he or she may be the only health professional in the area. Husband-wife teams, for example, a nurse and a doctor, can also be more responsive to the health needs in an isolated area than can a single specialist. Being in good physical condition is also an advantage because it helps one avoid becoming physically run down with constant travel during harsh winters. One also may need strength to cope with a violent patient when the nearest help is a state trooper one day away by charter bush plane. Some counselors have even worked out rigorous training programs for themselves, or have enrolled in karate classes, to develop and enhance their physical condition (Stillner, 1974).

Working With Native Regional Health Corporations

With such far-reaching political reorganization taking place in the state, nonnative counselors are learning to operate increasingly within the framework provided by native regional health corporations (Bloom & Richards, 1974). Such new roles as trainer/trainee, counselor, broker/organizer/ health politician, and systems clinician are emerging as counselors attempt to work within the new structure.

TRAINER/TRAINEE.   One may need to be trained as well as to serve as a trainer for others. Some corporations are now organizing workshops with older people from the villages to learn about traditional forms of healing used in their region. Various training programs are being organized to train white "experts" about the cultural group with whom they will work. Nonnative counselors may be expected to work under the direction of native leaders or to work with native co-therapists to help adapt their general knowledge of counseling to the specific needs of the community. They may need to learn a whole new language as well as a new style of relating. In some parts of the state, shamans or local healers still practice, and much can be learned from working side by side with them.

In these sorts of programs, the only common denominator is the need for flexible, creative behaviors. Some counselors attempt to prepare themselves for these experiences through activities designed to sharpen their creative skills—sculpture classes, photography, music, psychological "growth" exercises, and the like. Others take courses in grant writing, administration, or contracting, depending on what the situation will require of them (Sexton & Zinser, 1975).

To respond more effectively to the problems caused by cultural differences, nonnative counselors may seek to train native counselors to assist them. Efforts have ranged from attempts to train native para-professionals or auxiliary helpers to attempts to develop options within the state for advanced formal training of natives in mental health administration, medicine, and psychiatry (Schwarz, 1974). As a long-range strategy, preparing native counselors to assume professional responsibilities of various types is certainly needed. Counselors who wish to be involved in these areas, however, will often need more training themselves—in such subjects as cross-cultural education methods and curriculum design—before they can really implement their desires.

COUNSELOR.   This is the role that many readers may have expected to be the main subject of this chapter, that is, the role of a person who tries to help others through such counseling techniques as talking with another person, providing support, attempting to give insight, and so on. However this is just one of the many functions that are included under the title *counselor.* For nonnative counselors, at least, this sort of work may be only a small part of their total role, since they will often find it more effective to have para-professionals perform these tasks than to do them directly.

Even when counselors do these more traditional counseling activities directly, however, they may have to make major changes in their methods. For example, a patient who has overdosed and needs an emergency medical checkup may be located in a village 1,500 miles from the nearest hospital, with the telephone system inoperative because of bad weather. Or a patient may barricade himself or herself in a house and threaten to use a gun if he or she is bothered. Obviously, a "counselor" called on to help in these kinds of cases is going to be in trouble if he or she says, "But I only do Gestalt therapy," or has some other limited conception of his or her role. Many psychological concepts such as transference or acting out seem rather academic when one is struggling to disarm a violent patient. In these situations, what needs to be done may be clear, but improvising a way to do it may be difficult. There is no substitute for experience, and counselors can gain experience only by paying their dues by working at least several years in Alaska.

Because of transportation and communication problems and lack of professional resources, it may be possible to see a client only a limited number of times. Self-help methods can be useful for such individuals. For example, clients can be encouraged to express themselves through a variety of avenues—autobiographies, drawings, poems, dances—to gain as much insight as possible through self-analysis, and then be encouraged to develop their own treatment programs (Bloom et al., 1974).

Other helpful methods include crisis and brief treatment counseling. One can establish a treatment contract with some clients that sets a definite limit on how many times they will be seen, and outlines very limited objectives. One may also seek to identify the healthiest member in a given family and enlist that person's aid as co-therapist to help others in the family, and to follow up on the treatment plan after the counselor has flown away.

What the most effective counselors seem to have in common are not specific techniques but personal qualities such as warmth, a tendency to be action-oriented, a sense of humor, and enough flexibility to adapt to situations in which ordinary counseling rules may not apply (Kleinfeld, 1972a, 1972b). Such personal qualities may have little connection with formal education or schooling. And it is not enough for a counselor to try to mimic these kinds of personal characteristics. For example, a counselor who tries to smile a lot and act warmly toward a client when he or she does not really feel this way will be perceived by the client as nongenuine. Or a counselor who tries to help others when his or her own personal conduct does not exhibit much wisdom will not be thought effective by clients.

Because of the mixture of old and new in Alaska, many clients are ambivalent about counseling, simultaneously holding traditional and modern concepts and values about mental health. They may therefore consult modern counselors for some types of concerns, and local healers or wise people in their village for others. Moreover, nonnative counselors often serve in a variety of roles because of scarce professional resources. Thus it is not uncommon to have a patient who may also be one's boss in an organization, another who is one's student in a training program, and another who is a contractor receiving money from the counselor for a mental health project. Personal relationships over time seem to be the main therapeutic ingredient in such complicated interactions.

A major barrier may occur in counseling interviews when the differing value systems of counselor and client come into conflict. For example, assumptions about individual responsibility for behavior may vary from culture to culture. Many Alaska Natives seem to be especially sensitive to group processes, and often seem to prefer reliance on group solutions to problems rather than on individual solutions. A counselor who believes that a client should take individual initiative for handling his own concerns may tend to de-emphasize group or family solutions, without being fully conscious of what he or she is doing. Therefore when a client interprets the reason for part of his difficulties as somebody else's fault, the counselor with a more individualistic set of values would be apt to label this as projection. A client who is very closely attached to other family members and relies heavily on them for advice and support all of his life may seem dependent or immature to a counselor whose own culture discourages, and may even look with suspicion on, intense family ties.

Sorting out these issues is especially difficult in cases like that of the schoolgirl who had been bounced about from one foster home to another. Her misbehavior in school was partly the fault of others in the school and in the foster home system. It would be hard for a counselor, even one of the same culture, to help this girl sort out the projections and defensive rationalizations from the realities of her life. When the situation is further complicated by different cultural assumptions about individual versus group responsibilities, a counselor may find it next to impossible to reach the client effectively.

Another example of this same sort of dilemma concerns differing time values. People from villages where the pace of life is relatively slow may be put off by urban counselors used to tight time schedules and 50-minute hours. A client who comes late to appointments or who often misses appointments may simply not be proceeding at the same pace as the counselor. Then again, he or she may be angry at the counselor or feel that the counseling is not worthwhile. Or the client may simply be having realistic problems in arranging transportation and baby-sitting just to be able to appear at the counseling session.

Examples like these can be duplicated in a number of

areas. The important point is that when behavior does not fit what the counselor expects, the counselor may jump to the conclusion that the other person is exhibiting defensiveness, resistance, projections, lack of cooperation, or similar kinds of negative behaviors. The client may pick up these feelings from the counselor and begin to react to them, setting in motion a vicious circle in which lack of understanding escalates on both sides.

Counselors must therefore try to sensitize themselves to values implicit in their counseling style, and to be aware of potential conflict areas with clients from other cultures. The process of counseling people from other cultures tends in itself to highlight some of these value conflicts, and the counselor must attempt to keep communication lines open with the client and to avoid stereotyping or premature labeling of behavior as abnormal. Here again, consulting with relatives of the client or members of his peer group may prove invaluable in deciding what is or is not a problem. Would this particular person, from this particular subculture, feel more comfortable with a male or a female therapist? Is wife beating really a problem behavior for this particular patient from this particular subgroup? These are the kinds of questions relating to basic values that a counselor in this sort of work soon learns to ask.

To complicate matters even more, nonverbal behavior may have quite different meanings in different cultures. Again, the number of possible variables makes generalizations difficult. An experienced counselor, however, can sometimes establish communication with a native patient in a way that will seem almost miraculous to a less experienced counselor. When asked to describe the secret of success, the counselor may often be hard-pressed to put it into words. Often the nonverbal behaviors—body position, facial expressions, rhythm and tone of speaking, type of eye contact—are the critical factors in putting a given client at ease and helping him or her communicate more easily.

Some experts on nonverbal communication have estimated that 80 to 90% of all communication takes place nonverbally (Birdwhistell, 1970). One can see the special importance of nonverbal behavior in Alaska, where language barriers are often a given, and the counselor frequently finds himself or herself trying to work with an untalkative patient. The process of learning about these behaviors is similar to the process of learning a new language. First, one learns the words of the language, and only later does one learn the accents, intonations, and styles of phrasing that make one sound like a native. Correct accents are learned not by reading but by observing local people speaking and trying to mimic their phrasings and ways of speaking. In the same way, cross-cultural counselors need to cultivate the art of observation in these nonverbal areas, try to adopt some of them into their own style of behaving, and be aware of potential communication blocks that can result if they are misunderstood or misinterpreted.

A patient who had recently experienced the death of someone for whom she cared deeply came to group therapy sessions, but always seemed quite guarded. When the counselor urged her to express her feelings, she stopped coming to the group. She telephoned later to explain that she was afraid to return to the group because she might have broken down and cried, and then the other patients would have thought she was crazy. The counselor was caught completely by surprise, having had no clue that the patient was experiencing such feelings. His definition of appropriate and acceptable expressions of nonverbal behavior (working through grief by crying in public) had clashed with the patient's feelings that such actions in front of others would be very shameful. He had misread her reluctance to speak of her grief as guardedness, and had misjudged the degree of stress she was feeling by being in the group.

With time, this counselor learned to tune in with great accuracy to the nonverbal signals from similar patients, is now able to establish easy and immediate rapport with them, and has become most effective in helping them. When asked to define how he accomplishes this, however, he has difficulty. Again, the crucial factor appears to be sensitizing oneself to nonverbal cues so that one automatically reacts in a way that will facilitate communication. The literature on kinesics and the scientific study of nonverbal behavior is growing (Scheflen, 1972). But so far, Alaska Natives have not been included in such research. Counselors therefore need to become intuitive artists with their Alaskan clients and need to strive to decipher the nonverbal signals communicated by their patients.

BROKER/ORGANIZER/HEALTH POLITICIAN.   Another role about which counselors in Alaska need to be knowledgable is that of broker, organizer, or health politician. Because of the large numbers of federal and state funding sources for mental health programs in Alaska, it can be a full-time job just keeping track of various funds, helping Natives write grants to obtain these funds, or helping local groups in other ways to obtain mental health resources. Many counselors accordingly become a kind of middleman between funding sources and counseling programs. Often they are also involved as program administrators or as politicians trying to influence the development of certain types of programs. Again, because of the number and variety of programmatic efforts underway, a counseling program may have to compete with all sorts of other programs for funding. As a result, counselors tend to become more politicized than they might be in other parts of the country. A term beginning to appear in the literature for this sort of work is *culture broker* (Weidman, 1973; Lefley, 1974; Sussex, 1975).

SYSTEMS CLINICIAN.   A final role that can be identified for counselors working in the newly emerging health corporations is that of systems clinician (Curtis, 1973). The counselor tries to catalyze the group with whom he works into peak performance, to improve staff morale, increase productivity, and improve coordination with other programs. To accomplish these tasks, he or she may need to be continually switching gears—functioning at one moment as an individual counselor to a fellow staff member, at another time as a trainer, at still another time as an administrator or broker. Some systems seem to be "sick"—with high staff turnover, alienation or constant friction among staff members, goldbricking, or fragmentation of efforts. Other systems seem much healthier, with happy, productive staff. Some counselors seem to have the leadership abilities to be able to improve the health of the system in which they work; others do not.

This is another area that is difficult to describe precisely, but it is vital to an understanding of the kind of situation with which counselors in Alaska will need to cope if they are to be effective. The skill involved here has to do with combining very heterogeneous elements in a group of people into a blend that maximizes staff morale and productivity. Every ounce of one's clinical skills may be required for this type of activity, for the people one works with will consider themselves peers and resist any attempt to label them as patients or clients.

NEED FOR RESEARCH

Data are extremely scarce in virtually every area discussed in this chapter, and what statistics and studies there are on mental health in Alaska are open to a variety of interpretations. We need more research involving a very close collaboration among and between cultures in all phases of the study, to explore more systematically the frontier described here, where social psychology, cultural psychology, and applied counseling meet.

SUMMARY

Alaska has many unique features—vast area, ecological and cultural diversity, severely limited transportation and communication facilities, and a rapidly changing political and economic situation. Some sample counseling situations have been described to illustrate how these unique factors relate to the counselor's role. Also discussed were some approaches being developed to adapt counseling methods to this unique setting, methods to overcome transportation and communication problems, and some of the new roles and techniques used by counselors in the newly emerging native regional health corporations.

All in all, it is an exciting time to be a counselor in Alaska, but also a confusing and complex time, where many of the situations one encounters do not fit established theories or models of counseling.

REFERENCES

Age and sex characteristics of Alaska's population. *Alaska Review of Business and Economic Conditions,* 1972, *9*(1).

Alaska Native Claims Settlement Act. Washington, D.C.: House of Representatives Report No. 92–746, 1971.

Attneave, C. *Areas of basic research, relevant to racism and ethnicity, that could productively involve American Indians both as researchers and as subject populations.* Ford Foundation Task Force on Racism, 1973, (Mimeograph).

Birdwhistell, R. *Kinesics and context.* Philadelphia: University of Pennsylvania Press, 1970.

Bloom, J., Mendelsohn, B., & Richards, W. Experience statements of Alaska Native high school students. In *Proceedings: Third International*

Symposium of Circumpolar Health. Yellowknife, Northwest Territories, Canada, 1974.

Bloom, J., & Richards, W. Alaska Native Regional Corporations and community mental health. *Psychiatric Annals,* 1974, *4*(9), 65–75.

Coleman, R., Hopson, M., Matthew, S., & Peoples, T. *Some concerns of native people regarding mental health program development,* 1974, (Mimeograph).

Curtis, W. Community human service networks: New roles for the mental health worker. *Psychiatric Annals,* 1973, *3*(7), 23–42.

Federal Field Committee for Development Planning in Alaska. *Alaska Natives and the land.* Washington, D.C.: U.S. Government Printing Office, 1968.

Feigin, R. A grass-roots mental health program in Norton Sound. In *Proceedings: Third International Symposium on Circumpolar Health.* Yellowknife, Northwest Territories, Canada, 1974.

Kleinfeld, J. *Effective teachers of Indian and Eskimo high school students.* Fairbanks, Alaska: Institute for Social, Economic, Government Research, University of Alaska, 1972a.

Kleinfeld, J. *Interpersonal relationships across cultures. The selection of urban boarding home parents for Indian and Eskimo students.* Fairbanks, Alaska: Institute for Social, Economic, Government Research, University of Alaska, 1972b.

Kraus, R. Mental health program development in rural Alaska. In H. Resnick & H. Parad (Eds.), *Emergency mental health care in the U.S.* Philadelphia: Charles Press, 1976.

Lefley, H. *Implementation of culture brokerage and culture mediation in mental health care.* Presented at the 73rd annual meeting of the American Anthropological Society, Mexico City, November 19–24, 1974.

Public Law 93–638, 93rd Congress, S. 1017, January 4, 1975.

Scheflen, A. *Body language and social order.* Englewood Cliffs, N.J.: Prentice-Hall, Inc., 1972.

Schrader, J. *Observations on the mental health system of the state of Alaska,* 1973, (Mimeograph).

Schwartz, R. WAMI: An experiment in regional medical education. *Western Journal of Medicine,* 1974, *121*, 333–341.

Sexton, H., & Zinser, E. *A survey of Alaskan continuing education needs in mental health,* 1975, (Mimeograph).

Stillner, V. Adaptational experiences in an extreme environment. In *Proceedings: Third International Symposium on Circumpolar Health.* Yellowknife, Northwest Territories, Canada, 1974.

Sussex, J. (Ed.). Psychiatry and the social sciences. *Psychiatric Annals,* 1975, *5*(8).

Time Magazine. Issue on the Alaska pipeline, June 1975.

Weidman, H. *Implications of the culture broker concept for the delivery of health care.* Paper presented at the annual meeting of the Sourthern Anthropological Society, Wrightsville Beach, N.C., March 8–11, 1973.

Wilson, M., & Brady, C. *Health care in Alaska via satellite,* 1975, (Mimeograph).

Chapter 3

BLACK PERSPECTIVES ON COUNSELING

William David Smith

Because of a variety of historical and cultural factors, blacks cannot be effectively counseled by using the same techniques that are appropriate for white clients. Counselors, especially white counselors, must overcome their biases and develop a genuine understanding of the special needs of black clients.

INTRODUCTION

The phone rang. Seconds later I was informed that it was for me. The voice on the other end asked if I would write a piece on counseling blacks. "Do you think that there are some different things that should be known when working with blacks?" The caller asked me a very important question. The voice continued: "Is the counseling process different for blacks?" I answered yes to both questions. By this time my mind was racing with thoughts on understanding the total situation centered around black Americans and counseling. What follows is an attempt to present the main issues that one is likely to encounter when dealing with the topic of counseling black Americans.

I shall begin by trying to give the reader a brief history and overview of the vocational guidance movement and some of the movements of black Americans since 1619.

Neither time nor space permits a detailed historical account of both movements. However I hope that a succinct review will give the reader some idea of the progress made by each movement. In my opinion it is difficult to analyze the problems or concerns encountered in counseling black Americans without reviewing both movements.

This will be followed by a discussion of educational training programs for counselors, the counseling process, things counselors should know as they work with black clients, and a set of recommendations.

TERMINOLOGY

I have not used such terms as culturally deprived, or culturally disadvantaged, or culturally different, or culturally underprivileged, or inner city residents, or cultural minorities, or urban disadvantaged, or societal minorities, or low-income residents, or colored folks, or people of color, or Afro-Americans to denote people of African descent. I am painfully aware that a large portion of the people of African descent prefer to be labeled Negroes. Another large portion of the people of African descent have decided to label themselves blacks. Still another segment of the people of African descent really do not seem to care what the whole thing is all about. Nevertheless, I have chosen, throughout this article, to refer to the people of African descent as blacks or black Americans. My reasoning is simple: I refer to myself this way.

HISTORY

Guidance

Guidance, of which counseling is a part, has been a natural, everyday process in the life of the family for hundreds of thousands of years. White families, generally, and black families, specifically, did what they had to do according to the norms of society.

In 1881 a little book was published that is perhaps the first book wholly devoted to the subject of choosing a vocation. Lysander S. Richards, the author, attempted to coin the word *vocophy* for the title. The tone of the book can best be demonstrated by extracting a piece from the preface:

> All we claim to perform is to bring order out of chance and chaos and form or establish a system to enable a person to find the most fitting pursuit in which he can reap the greatest success that is possible for him individually to attain (Brewer, 1918).

This book does nothing more than point out the need for vocational guidance. There is no mention of any type of guidance for blacks, who were then known as colored folks, Negroes, and niggers. Richards made few provisions for investigating occupations and, even in his study of the individual (excluding blacks), he talks primarily about what occupations to avoid, rather than which ones to follow.

Professional literature mentions the city of Boston most frequently as "the cradle of vocational guidance" (Humphreys, 1954). An experiment in Boston sponsored by a wealthy philanthropist, Mrs. Quincy A. Shaw, and directed by Frank Parsons, introduced the first nationally recognized program in guidance. This was the Bread Winner's Institute, organized in 1905–1906. Through this organization, Parsons began to develop vocational guidance on the basis of a planned program. He stated the basic principles of this program in a book, *Choosing a Vocation* (Humphreys, 1954).

In 1908 Parsons used the term *vocational guidance* and gave his official title as *director and vocational counselor*. It is said that this was the first time on record that the terms *vocational guidance* and *vocational counselor* were used.

Just as Richards made no reference to race, Parsons does not discuss vocational guidance or vocational counseling for black Americans. It is quite possible that both men either ignore the race question or believed, as so many people have for years, that whatever works for whites will also work for blacks. Other movements of the early 1900s were the mental hygiene, child guidance, psychology and educational, and economic or labor movements. Guidance and counseling as we know it today has drawn from the knowledge and techniques that were developed by these related movements. More specifically, the central core or foundations of most programs in counseling and guidance are based on (1) theories of personalities, (2) theories of learning, (3) theories of vocational choice, (4) measurement and evaluation, and (5) practicum experiences.

All of the teachings and learnings that are imparted to the student or future counselor traditionally originate from the areas just cited. In every instance, so far as I am aware, these subject matters were developed according to the norms of white society by white professionals with no real consideration given to the behavior of black Americans.

Concomitantly, as the vocational guidance movement was developing, and as other related movements were lending their concepts to educational institutions that train future counselors, there also developed the need to admit candidates to these programs. Admissions personnel in higher education elected to use screening tests to select program candidates. Because admissions personnel for most counseling and guidance programs were white, they have regularly employed tests based on the majority population. The problem is that it has been assumed that these "admission tests," usually the Graduate Record Examinations (GRE) or the Miller's Analogy, predict the success of black graduate students also. This assumption is erroneous. The best single predictor of future academic success is past academic performance, i.e., GPA. However, many blacks who have high GPAs have been denied admission to counseling and guidance programs because their test scores did not satisfy the personnel in the office of admissions. This, then, is a general account of the vocational guidance and related movements, and of the acute problem of the admission committee.

Black Americans

Most scholars of black history agree that in August 1619, when Captain John Rolfe exchanged human cargo for food, and Antony, Isabella, Pedro, and 17 other Africans stepped off the ship in Jamestown, Virginia, the history of black people in America began. For well over the next four decades, there was no racially-based class system. Together, blacks and whites lived, worked, died, accumulated land, voted, and owned servants, among other things. Blacks owned black and white servants, just as did whites.

Many historians believe that problems began for black Americans when decisions had to be made about who were to be the servants. The need for labor had increased because of the increased demand for cotton and tobacco throughout the world. Profit-oriented people asked, "How can we force people to work?" The answer was not simple. Indians and whites were both tried as servants. Indians were abandoned because they easily became ill, and whites were also abandoned as servants because they often ran away and easily blended in with other whites who were either masters, plantation owners, or freemen. After the use of these two groups of people failed, the spotlight was focused on the American blacks, who were, at the time, Africans. Blacks were used because they were strong, their color made it impossible for them to blend into the mainstream, and they were plentiful—that is, they were easy to get from Africa. Thus the rulers of early America established laws to make blacks permanent servants. Virginia and Maryland led the way in the 1660s. With the establishment of these laws, Virginia and Maryland set the legal precedent that influenced the lives of black and white Americans for well over the next two centuries. And for well over the next two centuries, blacks experienced conditions more dehumanizing than any in the history of this country, and perhaps the world (Bennett, 1969).

Blacks were raped of their history and culture; were told that they were worthless; were told they had no legal rights; were lynched; were forced to hate other blacks; were told they should not or could not own property; were told that they were lazy and uneducable; and were discriminated against in the educational system, the economic system, the religious system, the psychological system, the medical system, the political system, and the social system. It is against this background of deceit, oppression, misuse, exploitation, enslavement, court battles, sit-ins, freedom marches, freedom rides, jail-ins, stand-ins, marches on Washington; of witnessing the killings of common black Americans, such as the Tils, the Parkers, the Chaneys; of witnessing the killings of noted black Americans, such as Medgar Evers, Malcolm X, Dr. Martin Luther King, Jr.; of witnessing the killings of white people who tried to help black Americans, such as M. Schweiner, Anderson Goodman, Mrs. Viola Luizzo, John Kennedy, and Robert Kennedy; of participating in "black is beautiful" movements; and of watching white public officials in the nation's capital cut or eliminate federal and local programs that are designed to help black Americans, that we, blacks and whites, have arrived where we are in the United States today.

COUNSELOR EDUCATIONAL TRAINING PROGRAMS

Generally, counselor education has provided trainees with few or no educational courses that deal with counseling black Americans. Almost always, as we discussed in the foregoing section on the history of the vocational guidance movement, the graduate schools teach techniques and impart information that has been proven to work with whites, and assume that such techniques and information will be equally relevant to blacks. Such assumptions have proven to be false.

Counselors are taught by the traditionalists that the black client's concerns can be labeled as vocational, personal, educational, or social. Because counselors rely on previous training when counseling black clients, they (especially white counselors) discover that what they have been taught does not permit them to work successfully with their clients. Counselors learn that (1) their theory courses are obsolete, (2) they have not been given the kind of practical experiences needed to understand black clients, and (3) their experiences with tests in graduate schools do not help them to deal effectively with black Americans (Gunnings, 1971; Bell, 1971; Mitchell, 1971).

COUNSELING PROCESS

We have reviewed the vocational guidance movement and have seen that in the development of that movement there was "inadequate or no concern given to black Americans." We have also reviewed the history of blacks in America for well over three centuries and the resulting evidence also suggests that "inadequate or no concern has been given to black Americans." And we have reviewed graduate training programs in counselor education, again finding that "inadequate or no concern has been given to black Americans."

Is it any wonder that many counselors in elementary school, junior high school, high school, college, and in the community exhibit little concern for black Americans? Are these counselors, whether black or white, just a reflection of the values of the larger society? The obvious answers are "no" to the former question and "yes" to the latter.

We have seen, from the evidence presented in this paper, that the experiences of black Americans have been and continue to be different from the experiences of white Americans. Thus counselors, both black and white, must necessarily have some experiences in their graduate training that will make it possible for them to relate positively to their black clients. Later in this article, I shall advance a set of recommendations for all counselors and counselor education programs. For the moment, let me raise a key question and propose some answers. What are some of the things that counselors should know when counseling black clients?

All counselees are the sum of their experiences. All counselees bring their experiences to the counseling setting. In all probability, the future experiences of black counselees in America will continue to be different from the experiences of white counselees in America. As a result of these different experiences, blacks develop a different set of values, needs, aspirations, cultures, and outlooks on life. Despite what some counselors may have been told or may believe about black counselees, the facts are that all blacks *do not* think alike, look alike, sing, dance, play sports, and so on. Blacks are individually different. It follows that if counselors are to be successful with black counselees, they should use the "different model" not the "deficit model" when interacting with black clients. Counselors must do whatever is necessary to achieve a successful relationship with black counselees.

COUNSELORS NEED CSBKS

What is CSBKS? I think that all counselors should have or learn how to acquire what I call "Counselor's Sensitivity and Black Knowledge Style." CSBKS is especially important for all counselors who are working with black clients. If counselors have CSBKS and the usual competence to deal with personal, social, vocational, and educational problems or concerns, then they are likely to be useful and successful when counseling black Americans. If counselors have CSBKS and not the usual competence, they probably will achieve some success but should return to school to get the necessary information to become more proficient. However, if a counselor does not have CSBKS while working with black counselees, failure is inevitable.

Does the race of the counselor make a difference when working with black counselees? Yes! But black and white counselors must possess CSBKS if they are to succeed with black counselees. Black counselees can more easily identify with black counselors than they can with white counselors. Thus the black counselor is more likely to have a positive relationship and a better outcome with a black client than a white counselor. However, if a black counselor apes the traditional white counselor, then the outcome will probably be failure.

What does the research indicate? The literature reflects a dearth of research (although there have been many discussions) about the impact of race on counseling. However the literature raises two questions that are relevant to this paper: (1) What effect, if any, does the race of the counselor have on the interview behavior of black clients? and (2) What are black clients' racial preferences for counselors? The research on both questions was reviewed by Don K. Harrison (1975). Do white counselors achieve positive results when counseling black clients? Phillips (1960) researched this question and reported in his conclusion that white counselors could not counsel black students effectively. Adair (1972) found that black counselees expected white counselors to render less unconditional positive regard than black counselors.

Do black clients prefer black counselors or white counselors? In researching the relationship between what blacks prefer to be called and their preference for a black counselor, Jackson and Kirschner (1973) concluded that students who call themselves Afro-Americans or blacks had preferences for counselors of African descent more than those who referred to themselves as Negroes. Grantham (1970) reported in a racial study of client and counselor similarity that the black college students preferred black counselors over white counselors.

In another study, Banks, Berenson, and Carkhuff (1967) investigated the effects of counselor race and training on black counselees in the initial interview. Four counselors were involved in the study, one black and three white. Eight black counselees (four males and four females) were also part of the study. The investigators reported that all of the counselees indicated they would return to see the black counselor. Two-thirds of the counselees indicated that they would not return to see a white counselor.

In response to the two questions that were raised, the research indicates that (1) white counselors are not as effective in the counseling interview interaction with black clients, and (2) black counselees consistently prefer black counselors over white counselors.

WHAT ELSE DOES CSBKS ENTAIL?

Generally, counselors know that a requisite for a good relationship with their counselees (which leads to effective sessions) is the establishment of good rapport with their counselees.

CSBKS entails rapport. Rapport is defined as the ideal relationship between counselor and counselee (Arbuckle, 1965). It is the harmonious relationship that exists between the client and the counselor in the counseling dyad (Vontress, 1971).

CSBKS also involves understanding the possible language barrier. The basic tenet of counseling is based on the notion of the counselor and the counselee being able to communicate with each other. The spoken word is the main vehicle employed. If the people in the dyad cannot understand each other, then nothing is achieved and the counselee usually has an unpleasant experience and negative perceptions of counseling.

When I speak of counselors understanding black language, I certainly mean an understanding that is deeper than the vernacular, although the understanding of the vernacular is essential. For example, as a counselor you should understand the meaning of such words or phrases as: deuce and a half, dig it, brother, down, downer, grapes, here comes Abe, hit on, hog, hump, joint, later on, ride, shucking, split, stomps, strung out, the man, upper, wasted, and what's the deal. How many of these words do you know? Their meanings appear at the end of this article. Counselors must begin to understand, if they are really to help blacks, the theory of black communication. The theory "is a perspective; and it is therefore a comprehensive explanation of communication in Black America. . . . The constituents of the metatheory are a frame of mind, scope of context, structural code and delivery of message" (Asante, 1975). Those interested in more elaboration of this theory are referred to the original source.

CSBKS involves learning and understanding blacks' special community environment and the significance of the black community as it relates to the behavior of the black client in and out of the counseling situation. It is difficult, if not impossible, for a counselor to succeed with a black client to a significant degree unless he or she understands and appreciates those black environmental influences surrounding black Americans during their maturation.

It involves genuine empathy. This point is highly related to the preceding point. Some counselors, more whites than blacks, simply cannot identify with black clients. Other counselors, of both races, can empathize with black clients on an intellectual level. However there are few counselors who can empathize with blacks on an intellectual and a feeling level. Genuine empathy necessarily must include both. As you read this article, counselor, do you have genuine empathy?

It involves understanding the black client and the "hesitant self-disclosure" behavior. Many black clients and most black Americans keep their antennas out and functioning. Blacks, by nature of their survival experiences, have had to be cautious about exposing themselves to white people and, in some cases, to nonwhite people. Many black clients refuse to or are hesitant to expose themselves because they get bad vibes from their counselors from which they conclude that the counselors cannot help them or are unwilling to help them. Second, blacks must protect themselves or get ripped off. How do we know that this is true? The answer to this question is simple. Our life experiences have dictated this truth incessantly. Therefore many clients will never expose themselves to their counselors.

CSBKS involves understanding the meaning of "blackness." Blackness is a state of mind. It is the way *some* blacks have chosen to label themselves. The notion is that no one can label blacks, certainly not "the man," but blacks themselves. Generally, the term suggests that "black power had a few simple but powerful tenets for black people: (1) the United States of America is institutionally racist; (2) American society is materialistic; (3) America has a paternalistic attitude toward black people; and (4) black power believes that "'black is beautiful'" (Washington, 1968).

CSBKS involves the need for learning and understanding tests and blacks, as well as the ability and strong commitment to interpret test results as they relate to blacks. Counselors must be very sensitive to and knowledgeable about the way they handle test results with their black counselees. A case study follows.

A black graduate student at a predominately white university was called into the graduate office by the white admissions counselor. "Sit down," said the counselor, "I want to talk to you about your test results." The counselee sat down. The counselor explained, "The results of your test scores on the writing test are bad. You only scored at the fiftieth percentile. That means that you will have difficulty writing papers in your graduate courses. I recommend that you leave this university. It is too tough for you." Said the counselee: "I have been here for almost three quarters and have written 11 papers. I have received an 'A' on every paper." "Well," said the counselor, "you may make it but don't count on it." The student did graduate.

Intelligence and aptitude tests generally do not predict with any degree of accuracy the success of black people. Counselors must understand this as well as communicate it to the black client and others who are seeking test results about the client.

To some this information may seem unbelievable, to others it may seem typical, but to me it is a case of incessant racism that black Americans experience daily as we try to achieve. You see, I was that graduate student. For other information the reader is referred to Mathis (1969).

CSBKS involves understanding the black self-concept. This means that the counselor must promote and foster a positive self-concept for his black clients. He or she then strives to give the black clients good vibes about themselves. The counselor must free himself or herself from any hang-ups about the black client's self-worth. Black clients must be viewed externally on the basis of African heritage and not the European model. Thus the counselor, if he or she is to relate to black clients, must see the beauty in kinky hair, large noses, thick lips, black skin, and the black clients need to promote blackness.

It involves a thorough understanding by counselors that in American society most blacks must be bicultural in order to survive. And he or she must know when to use the knowledge to his or her advantage. The situation is certainly different for the American culture majority, who until recently knew almost nothing about black American life. White Americans have had to be only unicultural (Williams, 1971).

It involves the understanding by counselors of what Hayes and Williams, in separate works, refer to as the different model versus the deficit model of orientation. Counselors, especially white counselors, often view black clients as inferior rather than as different. Blacks are different because of the forced experiences to which we have been exposed from the American society (Hayes & Banks, 1972; Williams, 1971).

Finally, CSBKS involves being a black student advocate. The points listed above will not be effective unless the counselor is an advocate of black students on an unconditional basis (Williams, 1971).

What are some things that you as a counselor can do to acquire CSBKS? Several recommendations follow.

RECOMMENDATIONS

No set of recommendations that I could or shall advance can be substituted for the intuition about what works best with black clients under what conditions. Obviously, some techniques will work for some counselors and will not work for others. What is not so obvious is what techniques are needed for what counselors to be used with what black students. It becomes imperative, then, that counselors who work with racially different students develop a repertoire of appropriate counseling techniques. When dealing with black students, counselors should cease being similar to a *tabula rasa*. Counselors should build a mental file of techniques and ways to achieve success when working with black students. If their mental file is accurate and complete, then the selection of the correct file of information necessary to deal with black clients will be an easy and rewarding experience.

Just as the question of technique is not clear, it is also not clear what counseling style(s) should be developed by what counselors to be used with what black clients. Should counselors be passive, assertive, or aggressive when working with black students? Or should counselors try a combination of these? Each counselor must learn what techniques and styles are best to use when counseling blacks.

Below is a set of practical recommendations which, if implemented, will aid counselors in acquiring Counselor's Sensitivity and Black Knowledge Style (CSBKS), will aid counselors in their general understanding of key issues related to counseling blacks, and will be especially useful for white counselors.

Spot Counseling

Many black students do not necessarily come or care to come to the counselor's office. Therefore counselors can perform a service to black students by counseling or advising them on the spot. That is, counselors can help them wherever they are. Thus counselors can be effective in the hallways, on the playgrounds, and in some cases in the toilets or in the gyms after school; or at various athletic events, such as basketball and football games; or at various clubs, such as the French Club, or the Spanish Club; or just standing on the campus rapping. Of course, there may be times when you have to ask the client to come to your office. The obvious point here is that counseling can take place in a setting other than the counselor's office.

Employing Black Students

Black students are very sensitive. They are incessantly "checking out" counselors to see if counselors are sincere in their efforts to help them as they say they are. One of the best ways for counselors to get their messages across is to use black students in their offices as helpers. In the public schools no pay is necessary. If it is done correctly, black students will be honored to work in the office with the counselors. On the college level, some pay might be involved, but the dividends returned will make the small investment well worth the effort. Black students will tell other black students about the sincerity of the counselors in the office. Students tend to believe other students before they will believe counselors. A counselor's best bet is to develop black students who are counselor advocates.

Black Experience Appreciation

Counselors must develop a new "learning set" so that they can appreciate the black experience. Most counselors in the United States appreciate the white experience. Conversely, they have difficulty legitimizing the black experience. Counselors can learn to appreciate the black experience by understanding it. This means that special efforts must be made by counselors to read *many* books, papers, etc., about black life in America. Reading a few books will not be enough. If counselors learn to appreciate the black experience in America, they will in turn appreciate their black clients and thus be positive toward them. Hence they will be successful in most of their counseling relationships with black clients.

Another way to learn to appreciate the black experience is to enroll in a course for credit, such as black history or black literature. Counselors should encourage their black clients to enroll in courses in the black experience.

When counselors react negatively toward a black course they are also reacting negatively toward their clients, whether they know it or not.

Still another thing that counselors can do to gain an understanding and appreciation of the black experience is to attend specific functions that are important to blacks. Counselors should attend Dr. Martin Luther King Day programs, black history week programs, black cultural arts programs, black movies, black churches, and other black events. This type of behavior will unquestionably demonstrate to black clients that you as their counselor appreciate and understand what black people are all about.

Office Reading Material

All counseling offices should house black reading materials. Counselors should purchase *Jet, Ebony, The Black World, The Black Scholar, Essence, Black Sports,* black movie star magazines, black newspapers, and especially local black publications. This information should be available not only for black counselees, but for counselors as well. It is imperative that counselors read and be informed about what is important to the black community. Having material available in the counseling office will help black clients identify positively with the counseling office. And it will help the teaching staff learn about black people.

Special Conferences

Counselors should attend all conferences (or as many as budget will allow) that deal with counseling black students. White counselors who attend these meetings need to observe and listen more than they have at past conferences. White counselors also need to ask more questions about their "whiteness" as it relates to failure in their attempts to work with black students.

Black Acceptance

Counselors must accept black students as they are. They must accept black students who come to their offices with plaited or braided hair, with hats on their heads, with long Afros, with beards, with hip walks, with many finger gestures, with dashikis, with combs in their hair, with shirts outside of their pants, and with brightly colored clothing.

Immediate Gratification

Counselors should engage in counseling sessions with black clients that have fairly quick payoffs. Because of their experiences with the system, many black clients are tired of delayed gratification and therefore seek quick gratification of their chosen goals. Counselors must identify with these needs of their clients.

Black Vocational and Educational Counseling

Counselors, especially white counselors, should not prejudge what blacks can do when they are seeking jobs or when they are seeking college or other forms of post-high-school training. Counselors must be positive as they give advice to black youngsters. Many black students with average grades do quite well in their post-high-school training programs.

Counselee Preference

Black counselees specifically, and clients generally, should be given the opportunity to select their own counselor. The practice in most schools of assigning students to counselors by grade levels and not giving them any other options is in dire need of change. All educational settings should have black counselors and counselors of other minority groups in proportion to the school population to accommodate this choice.

Counselor Educational Training Program

The curriculum must be changed to include learnings that will help the counselor work effectively with black clients. Future counselors should be required to take courses in white racism, the black family, black identification, black history, the psychology of oppression, the black child, sociology and psychology of the black community, black psychological behavior, and the black woman. Counselors should also be required to gain some practical experience in the black community. If courses such as these were included in the curriculum of all counselors, the percentage of counselor failures with black clients would be drastically reduced.

Research

There is a need to conduct research and to establish some theories on black behavior, particularly by black psychologists (Chimezie, 1973). Personality theories advanced by Freud, Jung, Adler, Sullivan, Rogers, and others generally do not work with blacks. We also need theories of vocational choice that are more related to black Americans. There should be more information like that provided by Williams (1972).

Tests

More tests must be developed that accurately predict the black American's potential for success. This recommendation is extremely significant, albeit difficult to implement. The question that is asked so frequently is, What tests should be used with blacks? No one really seems to have the answer. Dr. Norman Dixon and Dr. Robert Williams of Pittsburgh and St. Louis, respectively, and others are doing research that is expected to answer this question more definitely. In the interim, many tests will be used with black Americans. During this period, how does one go about selecting tests that are suitable for blacks? One suggestion is to read through the manual and be certain that black experts have evaluated the items that are used. In some cases it may be necessary to write to the test publisher to ascertain whether or not you should use certain tests with blacks. A second suggestion is to use the Compendium of Tests (Samuda, 1975). Another suggestion is to consult with the Association of Black Psychologists by writing to the President at 14 T Street, N.E., Washington, D.C. 20017. Still another suggestion is to employ a black consultant to advise you on what tests should be used with blacks. This black test expert could also conduct workshops.

In-Service Training and Workshops

In-service training that deals with how to counsel black clients is needed immediately for counselors and counselor educators. These programs might consist of theory courses in the urban school of the 70s and 80s, black communities and the role of the counselor, and counseling black students and their parents. Field placement (all in inner city settings), practicum experiences (elementary, intermediate, and advanced), and group practicum experiences would be an essential part of such a program. The inner city experiences supplied to counselors through this program must be highly supervised.

It is imperative that the directors of such programs get concrete suggestions from the anticipated participants of these programs. Otherwise, not only is an important resourse lost completely or under-utilized, but the programs

may fail without this input. The selection of staff and participants is vital to the success of in-service programs; therefore careful screening of both groups is a must. I prefer a
year-long in-service training program; however this may
not be feasible for some. What is feasible for all, though,
is some type of program that helps counselors better
understand the black clients whom they counsel.

Race Counseling

More investigations are needed to isolate and quantify
those specific successful techniques employed by black
counselors as they work with black counselees. Similarly,
more studies are needed to determine the role of white
counselors with black clients. Can white counselors achieve
a minimal degree of success with black clients, or should
their role be "one of . . . change agent and interpreter in
the white community" (Kincaid, 1969)?

Institutes

Summer and year-long institutes that specifically prepare
counselors to work with black clients need to be established
immediately.

Recommendations Specifically for White Counselors

OPEN ADMISSION.   White counselors often do not hear
what their black clients are saying, and even those counselors who do hear, frequently do not *understand* what their
black counselees are saying. Counselors should use the
technique of repeating or summarizing what they think
they have heard their clients say. Counselors should wait
for verification from their clients before they proceed.
When a counselor does not know or understand where
black clients are coming from, they should openly confess

that they do not understand and ask their counselees to repeat or explain. Black clients usually know when their white counselors do not know what is happening in an interview anyway. Second, you must admit openly to yourself and to your counselees that in almost all cases, if not in all, black clients and black people in general know more about the black experience in America than white counselors and white people in general. This means that you can learn from your black counselees if you allow your client to act as teacher. This open admission will help you achieve greater success. Try it today.

MODELING.   White counselors should not refer to themselves or other whites as models for black clients, but should continually refer to black models for their black clients to emulate. And I do not necessarily mean referring to super blacks either. There are blacks who are successful, but who are not super.

OTHER SUGGESTIONS.   White counselors should:

1. Investigate their own historically rooted role in the vast amount of racism that exists in America today.
2. Create ways to combat rampant racism in the white community and in their work settings.
3. Request that black and African history and culture courses be taught in the school systems at every level.
4. Associate themselves with thinking black people who accept their own blackness. In this way white counselors will receive inputs that are different from those that they have traditionally received.
5. Recruit and hire better-trained white counselors who understand how to work with black people. This should be done only when it is impossible to find black counselors to work with black people.

6. Devise avenues by which both the image of black people, (especially the clients) not only among others, but also among themselves, will be improved. In completing this task, white counselors will change or improve their own images of black people.

7. Support organizations such as the Urban League, CORE, NAACP, SCLC, PUSH, and other local organizations that are fighting to improve the status of blacks in America.

8. Accept their own inadequacies as white counselors. Only in this way can they grow into better understanding of themselves in relationship to black people.

In summary, then, this paper has dealt with the history of the guidance movement and its relationship to blacks; the history of blacks in America since 1619; the counselor educational training programs; the counseling process; the counselors' need to acquire Counselor's Sensitivity and Black Knowledge Style (CSBKS); the reported research on two questions: (1) What effect does the race of the counselor have on black clients? and (2) What are the racial preferences of counselors by black clients? Finally, recommendations that will help counselors understand and work better with black clients were provided.

The words referred to earlier in this Chapter and their meanings are listed below.

Deuce and a half: a large Buick
Dig it, brother: I understand
Down: depressed
Downer: drugs that put you to sleep
Grapes: wine
Here comes Abe: a Lincoln

Hit on: to talk to or ask for
Hog: a Cadillac
Hump: working
Joint: marijuana
Later on: see you after awhile, or bye
Ride: any car
Shucking: a waste of time
Split: to leave
Stomps: shoes
Strung out: confused
The man: Caucasians
Upper: drugs that keep you awake
Wasted: drunk
What's the deal: how are you feeling

REFERENCES

Adair, R. G. *The effects of counselor-client differences in race of black clients' anticipation and perception of counselor behavior.* Unpublished doctoral dissertation, Auburn University, 1972.

Andrew, D., & Wiley, R. *Modern methods and techniques in guidance.* New York: Harper Brothers, 1955.

Arbuckle, D. S. *Counseling, philosophy, theory and practice.* Boston: Allyn & Bacon, Inc., 1965.

Asante, M. K. A metatheory for black communications. *Journal of Black Psychology,* February 1975.

Bancroft, J. F. Counseling the disadvantaged child. *School Counselor,* 1967, *14,* 149–156.

Banks, G., Berenson, B. G., & Carkhuff, R. R. The effects of counselor race and training upon the counseling process with Negro clients in initial interviews. *Journal of Clinical Psychology,* 1967, *23,* 70–72.

Banks, J. A., & Grambs, J. D. *The black self-concept implications for education and social science.* New York: McGraw-Hill, 1972.

Banks, W. M. The black client and the helping professionals. In R. Jones (Ed.), *Black psychology.* New York: Harper & Row, 1972.

Banks, W. M. *The differential effects of race and social class in counseling students.* Unpublished manuscript, University of California at Berkeley, Department of Afro-American Studies, 1971.

Barnes, E. J. Counseling and the black student: The need for a new view. In R. Jones (Ed.), *Black psychology*. New York: Harper & Row, 1972.

Bell, R. L. The culturally deprived psychologist. *The Counseling Psychologist*, 1971.

Bennett, L. *Before the Mayflower: A history of the Negro in America*. New York: Penguin Books, 1969.

Branson, B. D., & Monaco, D. A. Counseling in the urban setting. *Journal of the Association of Deans and Administrators of Student Affairs*, 1971, 170–175.

Brewer, J. M. *The vocational guidance movement*. New York: The Macmillan Company, 1918.

Burkett, L. S. *Race, ethnic attitude and verbal behavior*. Unpublished doctoral dissertation, Florida State University, 1966.

Burrell, L., & Rayder, N. F. Black and white students' attitudes toward white counselors. *Journal of Negro Education*, 1971, *40*, 48–52.

Carkhuff, R. R., & Banks, G. Training as a preferred mode of facilitating relations between the races and generations. *Journal of Counseling Psychology*, 1970, *31*, 412–418.

Carkhuff, R. R., & Pierce, R. Differential effects of therapist race and social class upon patient depth of self-exploration in the initial interview. *Journal of Counseling Psychology*, 1970, *31*, 632–634.

Chimezie, A. Theorizing on black behavior: The role of the black psychologists. *Journal of Black Studies*, September, 1973.

Clark, C. X., et al. Voodo, or I.Q.: An introduction to African psychology. *Journal of Black Psychology*, February, 1975.

Fitch, J. A. *Vocational guidance in action*. New York: Columbia Press, 1935.

Grantham, R. J. *The effects of counselor race, sex and language variables in counseling culturally different clients*. Unpublished doctoral dissertation, State University of New York at Buffalo, 1970.

Green, R. L. The awesome danger of intelligence tests. *Ebony*, August, 1974, 70.

Green, R. L. Tips on educational testing: What teachers and parents should know. *Phi Delta Kappan*, October, 1975, 89–93.

Gunnings, T. S. Preparing the new counselor. *The Counseling Psychologist*, 1971.

Harrison, D. K. Race as a counselor-client variable in counseling and psychotherapy: A review of the research. *The Counseling Psychologist*, 1975, *5*(1), 124–133.

Hayes, W. A., & Banks, W. M. The nigger box or a redefinition of the counselor's role. In R. Jones (Ed.), *Black psychology*. New York: Harper & Row, 1972.

Humphreys, J. A., & Traxler, A. E. *Guidance services.* Chicago: Science Research Associates, Inc., 1954.

Jackson, G. G., & Kirshner, S. Racial self-designation and preference for a counselor. *Journal of Counseling Psychology,* 1973 *20,* 560–564.

Jefferies, D. The needs of inner-city children for career guidance. *Elementary School Guidance and Counseling,* 1968, *2,* 268–275.

Jones, H. T. *The relationship of counselor-client personality similarity to counseling process and outcome.* Unpublished doctoral dissertation, University of Missouri, 1968.

Jones, M. H., et al. The neglected client. In R. Jones (Ed.), *Black psychology.* New York: Harper & Row, 1972.

Jourard, S. M., & Laskow, P. Some factors in self-disclosure. *Journal of Abnormal and Social Psychology,* 1958, *56,* 91–98.

Kincaid, M. Identity and therapy in the black community. *Personnel and Guidance Journal,* May, 1969.

Leacock, E. The concept of culture and its significance for school counselors. *Personnel and Guidance Journal,* 1968, *46,* 844–851.

Lewis, M. D., & Lewis, J. A. Relevant training for relevant roles: A model for educating inner-city counselors. *Counselor Education and Supervision,* 1970, *10*(1), 31–38.

Lewis, O. L., & Locke, D. W. Racism in counseling. *Counselor Education and Supervision,* 1969, *9,* 59–49.

Major, C. (Ed.). *Dictionary of Afro-American slang.* New York: International Publishers, 1970.

Mathis, H. I. The disadvantaged and the aptitude barrier. *Personnel and Guidance Journal,* January, 1969.

Millikin, R. L. Prejudice and counseling effectiveness. *Personnel and Guidance Journal,* 1965, *43,* 710–712.

Millikin, R. L., & Patterson, J. J. Relationship of dogmatism and prejudice to counseling effectiveness. *Counselor Education and Supervision,* Winter 1967, 125–129.

Mitchell, H. The black experience in higher education. *The Counseling Psychologist,* 1970, *2*(1), 30–36.

Mitchell, H. Counseling black students: A model in response to the need for relevant counselor training programs. *The Counseling Psychologist,* 1971.

Patterson, C. H. Counselor education for black counselors and for counseling black clients: Comments. *The Counseling Psychologist,* 1971.

Phillips, W. Counseling Negro pupils: An educational dilemma. *Journal of Negro Education,* 1960, *29,* 504–507.

Poussaint, A. F. The self-image of the Negro American. In Peter Rose (Ed.), *Old memories, new moods.* New York: Atherton Press, Inc., 1970.

Roussene, R. J. On racial gamesmanship and anti-intellectual attitudes in counselor education. *Counselor Education and Supervision*, 1971, *10*, 295–303.

Samuda, R. J. *Psychological testing of American minorities: Issues and consequences.* New York: Dodd, Mead & Company, 1975.

Sattler, J. M. Racial "experimenter effects" in experimentation, testing, interviewing and psychotherapy. *Psychological Bulletin*, 1970, *73*, 137–160.

Smith, D. H. Changing control in ghetto schools. *Phi Delta Kappan*, 1968, *49*, 451–452.

Smith, D. H. The white counselor in the Negro slum school. *School Counselor*, 1967, *14*, 268–272.

Smith, W. D. Black studies: A survey of models and curricula. *Journal of Black Studies*, March, 1971.

Smith, W. D. The black studies graduate in the "real world." *Personnel and Guidance Journal*, May, 1970.

Smith, W. D. Which way black psychologists: Tradition, modification, or verification-innovation? *Journal of Black Studies*, September, 1973.

Stranges, R., & Riccio, A. Counselee preference for counselors: Some implications for counselor implication. *Counselor Education and Supervision*, 1970, *10*, 39–46.

Thomas, C. W. *Boys no more: A black psychologist's view of community.* Beverley Hills, California: Glencoe Press Insight Series, 1971.

Vontress, C. E. Counseling Negro adolescents. *The School Counselor*, 1967, *15*, 86–91.

Vontress, C. E. *Counseling Negroes.* Boston: Houghton-Mifflin Company, 1971.

Vontress, C. E. Racial differences: Impediments to rapport. *Journal of Counseling Psychology*, 1971, *18*, 7–12.

Walker, J. M. *The effect of client race on the level of empathy of white counselor-trainees.* Unpublished doctoral dissertation, University of Illinois at Urbana-Champaign, 1970.

Washington, K. S. What counselors must know about black power. *Personnel and Guidance Journal*, November, 1968.

Wesson, K. A. The black man's burden: The white clinician. *The Black Scholar*, July–August, 1975.

Wigtil, J. An inner city institute: Observations of the director. *Counselor Education and Supervision*, 1971, *11*, 62–69.

Wilcox, R. C. (Ed.). *The psychological consequences of being a black American: A sourcebook of research by black psychologists.* New York: John Wiley & Sons, 1971.

Williams, R. L. The politics of I.Q., racism and power: An editorial. *Journal of Afro-American Issues,* Winter 1975, 1.

Williams, R. L. The silent mugging of the black community. *Psychology Today,* May 1974, 34.

Williams, R. L., & Kirkland, J. The white counselor and the black client. *The Counseling Psychologist,* 1971.

Willaims, W. S. Black economic and cultural development: A prerequisite to vocational choice. In R. Jones (Ed.), *Blacks psychology.* New York: Harper & Row, 1972.

Wolkon, G. H., Moriwaki, S., & Williams, K. J. Race and social class as factors in the orientation toward psychotherapy. *Journal of Counseling Psychology,* 1973, *20,* 312–316.

Young, A. H. *Race of psychotherapist and client and perception variables relevant to therapy outcome.* Unpublished doctoral dissertation, University of Illinois at Urbana-Champaign, 1972.

Chapter 4

PLANNING AND IMPLEMENTING TRANSCULTURAL TRAINING EXPERIENCES

Joyce M. Chick

Transcultural training experiences should be an important part of the staff development or counselor education program. Special considerations for planning such experiences are discussed in this chapter.

America has often been described as the "melting pot of the world" or as the "homogenized society." However there is ample evidence on radio and television broadcasts, in the newspapers, and in federal legislation of the past decade that this state of cultural unity has not been achieved. Although all minority groups are a part of American society, most remain apart from it. This fragmented social structure has resulted in cultural developments within the various subgroups of society that tend to make communication between these subgroups more difficult. One reason for this is the intolerance of anything different on the part of many people. An equally serious reason is the lack of a proper understanding of cultural differences, which is important to genuine communication. Even the most well-meaning people can lack this understanding.

Since their jobs require developing a deep level of communication and empathy with their clients, counselors need to pay particular attention to cultural differences and to how they may affect the counseling relationship. Transcultural training groups represent attempts to train counselors to deal with cultural differences by promoting understanding, sensitivity, and an awareness of how these differences affect interpersonal relationships. This chapter discusses means of planning and implementing such training experiences. These training groups need not be restricted to counselors, but are appropriate for teachers, para–professionals, administrators, and related professionals.

IN THE BEGINNING

There must be a seed of personal-professional motivation to plan and implement transcultural experiences. Ideally, this motivation will stem from the conviction that such experiences can bring about desired changes in people's understanding, attitudes, and behaviors. Transcultural behavioral changes can only come about through transcultural learning experiences—formal or informal. No amount of empathy, knowledge, or experience will ever enable an individual to transcend his own experience so completely that he can comprehend fully another person's life patterns, even in similar cultures. However we move closer to this knowing when we are able to share experiences with others, including all the aspects of their lives that verbal skills, body language, and the mental and emotional limitations of being human allow us to communicate. To this end, transcultural training experiences should afford individuals opportunities to come as close as possible to feeling what it would be like to live as a member of a different class or an ethnic group in our society, to be different from the majorities and from the "homogenized whole" of predominating cultural groups.

Historically, many of the laws of our society, as well as the traditions and cultural mores, reflect the cultural values and behaviors that have been developed by a Caucasian majority. Minority and ethnic populations have been either ignored or suppressed into silence until the last decade. Now these once voiceless groups are beginning to express themselves and to seek their right to human dignity.

To implement this process and promote progress, any of the following might be identified as target populations for transcultural training experiences: Mexican Americans, Eskimos, American Indians, Blacks, Cajuns of French ancestry in the Bayou country, Latin American immigrants (Chicano), Cuban exiles, and other ethnic populations such as the hyphenated ethnic groups, e.g., the Polish-Americans. All have at least three needs in common: (1) to be recognized as people with human needs; (2) to be understood in terms of their different cultural-ethnic heritages and to be helped in understanding the cultural-ethnic heritages of others; and (3) to be respected as people of dignity and worth.

In identifying transcultural target groups to be brought together, a second target population must also be identified, i.e., the professional group for which one wishes to provide transcultural training experiences. This group may consist of counselors training experienced counselors, or counselors functioning in large multiethnic school districts or areas in which integration programs or foreign immigration is occurring. The professional training group might include administrators, teachers, teams of pupil personnel workers, or any other mixture of professional workers who are providing helping services to ethnic groups. In some instances the professionals being provided the training experiences may themselves be members of ethnic groups.

It should be kept in mind that the composition of the training group will determine to a large extent the types of training experiences that should and can be provided. Although there may be some merit in mixing professionals within a training group (e.g., counselors with administrators), similar professional training work roles allow for the "Triple T" effect to occur as participants return to their regular jobs and share learned skills and changed attitudes with other professionals. Such spin-offs can be planned in the actual curriculum context of the transcultural learning experiences in the form of activities to be implemented in job settings. The impact of the training in their own work settings will be greater if training participants are selected from a small, well-defined geographic area, rather than from a widespread area. Five participants from the same school district should have greater impact on others in that area than five selected from five different school districts.

THE NEXT STEPS

Once the target populations have been identified, the next steps are critical to the outcomes and value of the training experience. Perhaps these steps can be most appropriately and explicitly outlined in questions that should be answered at this stage of the planning process.

Why Were These Particular Cultural Groups Identified?

Ethnic groups are generally selected in response to specific social and/or educational concerns that are confronting the school. These may be concerns with implementing racial or ethnic integration in a community or school and with providing helping personnel with the learning experiences and skills that will enable them to serve as facilitators in this process; there may be a sudden influx of an ethnic group that is creating community tensions in a predominantly Caucasian locale; or there may be an unanticipated outbreak of hostility between culturally different groups that had previously coexisted in relative peace. In addition, an awareness may come to exist of the value of transcultural training experiences as a way of promoting the social and educational welfare of minority group students, even in the absence of particular crises.

What Are the Major Objectives and Goals To Be Accomplished Through the Training Experience?

The changed or new behaviors that are desired should determine the objectives of the training experience. In planning, "objectives" are viewed as intermediate attainments that are projected toward more long range global behaviors or "goals." For example, a goal of a desegregation training institute might be to enable black and white counselors to broaden their knowledge of the black and Caucasian races in our culture, with particular emphasis given to cultural dissimilarities.

What Kinds of Learning Experiences Will Be Needed to Help Bring About the Desired Objectives and Goals?

The kinds of learning experiences that need to be provided for the participants are very directly related to the desired objectives and goals. I was involved in a training group in which three academic and practicum-based experiences were provided for the participants. A course taught by a black sociologist entitled *Sociology: Race and Culture* gave participants an academic basis for understanding racial issues in America. Each participant was allowed to develop a sociological case study through community contacts in homes of the other race. A practicum in *Interracial Group Processes* aided participants in experiencing each other as people of similarities and differences and in communicating across racial lines. An *Integrative Seminar* was designed to expose participants to current social issues and to allow for free-flowing discussions to enable the integration of many of the learning experiences taking place. Racially balanced *Personal Encounter Groups* provided opportunities for the participants to explore their attitudes, prejudices, and personal feelings toward themselves and each other. Without question, learning experiences in the affective domain are highly effective and extremely important for most individuals in transcultural training experiences. This is not to de-emphasize the value of cognitive learning experiences; however it is quite evident from previous training programs that individuals need help in exploring their personal value systems. Learning experiences in the affective domain help persons to get in touch with their own belief systems and to take ownership of their own behaviors. In transcultural workshops or institutes, it is often necessary to design special curricula utilizing a wide variety of human resources as well as material, field, and community resources. In this respect the workshop or project director has the opportunity to be both artist and architect, creating and planning toward specific outcomes.

How Can the Training Experiences Be Most Effectively and Accurately Evaluated?

The success of a program is a measure of how well its objectives have been met. If the objectives are well defined and measurable, the program's success, or lack of it, can also be measured. Care should be taken that the evaluation methods are appropriate to the parameter being evaluated. A variety of methods can be used including open-ended questionnaires, objective tests, point-rating scales, personal interviews, judge's panels of audio and video performance, recordings, and peer and trainer ratings.

What Kinds of Followup Activities Should Be Planned as Postevaluation Measures?

Finally, followup activities can be of immeasurable value as a sharing and learning activity for the participants when they are brought back together for a 2- or 3-day postsession. Enthusiasm for such an opportunity is likely to run high among the trainers and the participants. Indeed such an experience can be heart warming as well as intellectually rewarding. Such an activity should be scheduled 3 to 6 months after the original program. This gives the participants enough time to implement what they have learned as well as to integrate their training experiences. By all means have recording equipment available to use in postfollowup sessions, because it is here that growth and wisdom may unfold, spurred by the excitement of comradeship returned and skills that have now been field-tested. It is also in postevaluation sessions that participant feedback can enable the planners to appraise which were the most or the least meaningful training experiences. This feedback can also provide a sound information base to be taken into consideration in planning more effective training experiences for the future.

PLANNING AND ORGANIZATIONAL STRUCTURE

In the planning and implementing of any type of educational program, administrative management, organization, and structure are important for successful outcomes. These facets take on even greater importance when more intense and compact types of learning experiences are being planned and implemented, as is often the case in transcultural workshops. In fact the key to success in many endeavors is coordination.

At this point administrative leadership and administrative management should be differentiated. Management is the establishment and supervision of operational processes that emanate from the ideas, philosophies, creativity, and intellectual pursuits found in leadership. Although the two are often inextricably entwined, one should not be mistaken for the other.

Effective leadership is the seed component, as well as an ongoing ingredient in planning for and carrying out a transcultural learning experience. What, then, are the nuts and bolts that must be the concern of administrative management in such programs?

Essentially, the planning and implementation of a transcultural workshop or institute can be divided into three broad categories to reflect needs in administrative management: (1) planning and organizational structure, (2) program operation, and (3) program evaluation and followup. Categories two and three have already been discussed. Therefore it seems appropriate to direct attention to category one: planning and organizational structure.

What Does It Cost and Who Pays for It?

A major consideration that generally comes to everyone's attention very early and very quickly is how such learning experiences can be financed. Education is costly, and unique workshops or institutes usually require special funding.

There are a number of ways to meet the costs of such programs, and possible funding sources should be identified and explored in the very early stages of planning. The types of funding that may be available, in the absence of internal resources, include awards or grants from private foundations, business corporations, professional organizations, state legislative programs, and programs operated by the federal government. Federal funds may be allocated to states or grants administered at the state level. Directories of funding sources are usually available in university libraries and offices of public school systems. The federal government also sends out announcements of funds available under specific titles or acts and announcements for special projects they wish to fund to meet specifically identified societal needs. If outside funding is not sought to support special training programs, there are several other options. The cost of a program could be prorated to the participants in the form of a tuition. Another option, though not one of high probability in days of austerity, is support through in-service training budget allocations within educational systems.

The cost of such training programs will be directly affected by the resources available without cost in the system in which they are offered. For example, a large university or a large city public school system would logically have many internal resources upon which to draw charged costs. These funds are often referred to as "in-kind" or internal matched resources.

Although it is impossible to identify all expenses that should be included in budget planning for such special programs, one might wish to consider the following as potential costs:

Physical space
Special equipment (video, audio, etc.)
Instructional staff salaries and matching benefits
Special consultants and lecturers
Secretarial and support staff
Administrative staff and overhead
Instructional materials, books, and supplies
Office materials and supplies
Extracurricular activity funds

Stipends for participants
Travel and per diem for participants, faculty, and consultants
Printing, publications, and publicity
Needs for local transportation

In budgetary planning, expenses to be incurred during preplanning and postevaluation periods should not be overlooked, because these too require personnel and resources.

Selecting the Participants

The selection of participants for a transcultural training experience is directly related to identified needs and the desired goals. It may also be related to a geographic locale and to a specific concentration of ethnic groups. It seems logical to assume that such training experiences would be designed not only to facilitate change in the participants, but also to train them to be facilitators of change.

Other factors that may be considered in the selection process include: participant mixtures, e.g., two or more ethnic groups; educational fields and levels of specialization and training; employment settings; age and sex; and, when necessary, institutional admission requirements.

It has been helpful in prior selection processes to request brief summaries from applicants explaining why they wish to participate in the training experience.

Publicity

Publicity should serve two very well-defined purposes: to inform and to create interest and awareness. Once a special training program has been designed and funded, it should be publicized to target populations to inform and enlist the interest of potential applicants. This can be achieved through letters of announcement, specially designed brochures with tear-off return slips requesting applications, announcements in professional journal, newspaper feature articles, and radio and television stations which will often allot time as a community service.

Newspaper feature stories and radio and television are the most effective means of communicating with the general public; however announcements can also be made in civic clubs and at various other public meetings. The value of informing the general public is in creating a heightened awareness of special social issues and concerns and of existing efforts to alleviate them.

Publicity should not end with pre-announcements. Some of the activities in the ongoing training experience will frequently be of general public interest. Followup publicity can also be valuable in any of the previously mentioned media or in the form of professional publications. The latter may be formal summary reports for externally funded projects or articles for professional journals.

In the zeal of personal motivation and belief in what we are doing, it is often easy to forget that most of the real meaning resides within us—the doers. The trick is to share this meaning and awareness with others. The only means to this end is in clarity of communication, an often elusive accomplishment but one worth striving toward.

Physical Facilities

The types of training experiences one wishes to offer determine the types of physical facilities needed. One should distinguish between those facilities that are highly essential to accomplishing instructional goals and those that are highly desirable to the physical comfort and emotional attitudes of the participants.

Experience suggests that a "home-base room" reserved exclusively for participants in the training program is essential. This room can also serve as a general resource room where materials can be displayed, distributed, exchanged, and utilized, and where participants can congregate in unscheduled time to exchange ideas and cultivate personal and professional interactions. Daily announcements, calendars, and appointments can also be posted in specified locations. This room should become the hub of workshop activity and should house a special resource library.

Other types of physical facilities that should be considered may include video and audio rooms for individual and group observation and participation; small group meeting rooms; faculty offices for work preparation and conferences; and classrooms of various sizes.

Accessibility to meeting rooms for physically handicapped participants is a frequently forgotten consideration.

Schedules: Clock and Calendar

Special training programs frequently are offered in the summer in 3-, 5-, 6-, or 8-week courses. The job commitments and geographic locations of the target participants determine to a large extent when, where, and for how long training programs can be effectively offered. These factors can be accommodated by holding training sessions on weekends or evenings. Outreach programs also require special scheduling considerations because they usually take place in the work setting of the target population during work hours.

If participants are to be reimbursed for travel, thought must be given to the training site in budget construction.

Training programs in which participants attend full-time often tend to be intense and highly demanding. There is a mental and physical limit to what a learner can absorb and emotionally cope with in highly value-laden training experiences. Caution should be exercised to avoid going beyond this saturation point.

Scheduling that incorporates and coordinates both structure and flexibility is extremely desirable. The structure should provide the direction for and shape the activities of the training sessions, but flexibility is needed to accommodate particular needs that may arise during the course of the sessions.

Using Consultants

The use of consultants has closely paralleled the flow of federal dollars in the past decade. Before this period the invited expertise of the consultant was indeed a special privilege for all concerned. As external funding for education is now decreasing in proportion to national austerity, so too are the freedom and financial resources to use consultants.

Consideration should be given to state and federal agencies, as well as to national organizations, which will frequently provide special consultants without cost or for only travel reimbursement. The expertise available in local civic groups and community organizations and within local educational institutions could also be implemented effectively. The use of outside paid consultants is justified when the desired expertise that is needed is not available internally, when there is a person in the identified speciality who is known to be outstanding, and when the objectivity of a person external to the training system is desired.

Experience in administering transcultural training workshops indicates that careful consideration should be given to coordinating and sequencing consultants into the regular program. Consultants should fit into the training sequence in a natural and related way. Therefore the timing and planning for their participation is important.

Extracurricular Activities

It is highly important to plan social interaction activities in transcultural training experiences. Should the participants themselves be from selected ethnic groups, it is all the more important to provide opportunities for interaction outside the formal learning environment. It is here that many mythical stereotypes can be broken down.

In a previously mentioned desegregation training institute that had 15 white and 15 black counselor participants, it was discovered that most of the whites had never been inside a black person's home and that none of the blacks had ever eaten a meal in a white person's home. None of the participants had ever walked on public streets with someone of the other race.

One of the activities for this training was an invitation to the whole group to the home of a black professor for watermelon cutting and a picnic. It seems worth sharing that at this event a black female spit out a watermelon seed that was a bull's-eye to the forehead of a white male counselor who was also a practicing minister from a small rural community where congregations were indeed segregated. A chase began between the two in fun and jest, and resulted in both tripping over each other and falling to the ground. Laughter was everywhere and suddenly the white counselor realized this fun was OK. He looked up in astonishment and said, "Why don't you come hear me preach next Sunday? I've got a feeling worthy of a sermon about human beings." It was at this activity that the whites realized that blacks also have nice homes and attractive, clean bathrooms.

Lunch hours also provided opportunities to eat in mixed racial groups in public establishments. Dormitory housing for all who desired it was also arranged by racial mixtures.

To experience is to begin truly to internalize what the mind may have known but the human emotions have refused to acknowledge in feelings and behaviors. The four walls of a classroom can frequently be a very constrained learning environment.

The Learning Atmosphere

In conducting transcultural training experiences, every effort should be made to provide an atmosphere for learning that is as nonthreatening as possible. Just the title *transcultural* or the words *ethnic* or *racial* can carry charged emotional overtones for some individuals. Although the true test of the meaning of words is not so much how we use them as what we do about what they convey, participants all have their personal semantic wonderlands. Hopefully the training experience will alleviate some of the word association fears that are frequently related to stereotyped images.

Other fears may be associated with participation in affective learning experiences, such as personal growth groups or mixed ethnic discussion groups. In fact a person may experience fear just in attending and being a part of an ethnic blend. Time, exposure, and experience usually lessen all of these fears if an atmosphere of patience, warmth, and acceptance can be maintained.

Instructors and workshop leaders must make every effort to remain aware of the group's pulse beat and the tenor of the experience as it progresses. It may be necessary to alter or develop new strategies and learning experiences if the training sessions become too threatening. Although a degree of anxiety can facilitate learning, intense fears can literally paralyze effective learning. A delicate balance must therefore be sought.

Epilogue to a Prologue

The greatest value that could possibly be derived from this summary of thoughts and ideas is that they might serve as a beginning for others in planning and implementing transcultural training experiences. Although this nation has made great technological and scientific strides, there is still a human need to help people grow in their acceptance, caring, and love for each other. A personal definition of acceptance is feeling tolerance and a willingness to give recognition to others. Acceptance does not necessarily mean approval, but it does imply being open to and recognizing others.

Gilbert Wrenn writes that "your own perception of caring is a reflection of the person that you are." There are hundreds of definitions of caring, but I define it as an extension and giving of one's self to others. In greater depth, caring is not without respect for self, but it is without thoughts related to self.

The most complex and least understood of all human feelings is love. Wrenn cites Robert Heinlien's definition which well reflects a meaning appropriate to the present context: "Love is that condition in which the happiness of another person is essential to your own." Wrenn then asks the question: "Do we care for another because we should or because we cannot help caring?"

Transcultural learning experiences may provide bridges to acceptance in helping people to discover that the happiness of others is essential to their own. Epilogues to transcending cultural barriers are not yet ours, but prologues are ours for the caring.

REFERENCES

Chick, J. M. *Technical report of a special desegregation training institute for counselors: Race, culture, and interracial group processes.* U.S. Department of Health, Education and Welfare, Office of Education. P.L. 88–352, Title IV.

Heinlien, R. *Stranger in a strange land.* New York: Medallion Books, 1968.

Wrenn, G. C. *The world of the contemporary counselor.* Boston: Houghton-Mifflin Co., 1973.

Chapter 5

PLANNING AND LEADING TRANSCULTURAL GROUPS

Clell C. Warriner

We all lead groups. We all experience in some way in our associations with others the feeling of providing direction or making decisions for a group. Classes, teams, staffs, counselors and clients, families, dinner companions, gatherings of friends or coworkers, and clubs of various kinds are all groups. In this paper I have been asked to share what I know about planning and leading groups in general, with attention to transcultural groups in particular. Transcultural means across ethnic, racial, or socioeconomic boundaries, and almost everyone, in some aspect of his or her life, belongs to a transcultural group that fits this basic definition.

Transcultural means communication across differences in age, religion, intelligence, mental stability, sex, education, financial status, occupation, and marital status, differences in physical characteristics like height, weight, and visual and auditory acuity, as well as differences in culture. Every group is transcultural in that the members of every group have hundreds of similarities and differences, both actual and imagined. If a group leader makes the error of approaching a multiracial or multiethnic group as though that difference were the only or even the most important dimension of difference within the group, he is asking for trouble. In every group people arrange themselves and each other along a variety of different dimensions: the insider and the outsider, the talkative and the quiet, the thin and the fat, the dark and the light, the intelligent and the dull, the old-timer and the newcomer, the well-spoken and the halting, the private person and the sharer, the poet and the pragmatic, the outgoing and the shy, the beautiful and the ugly, the rebellious and the conforming, the braggart and the humble.

Knowledge of a person's cultural or ethnic background does not enable one to predict accurately where that person belongs in any of the above dimensions. An individual's view of himself varies depending on his or her personality and the context or frame of reference within which he is functioning. There is no such thing as a homogeneous group—there are only greater or lesser degrees of variance among group members.

Therefore my goal in this chapter is to set forth in a useful way some ideas about planning and running groups, as well as to describe some techniques that I have found especially useful in groups troubled by serious communication problems between and among participants (members and leaders). Although the focus will be on transcultural groups from the traditional definition of the word, it is hoped that the reader will find the principles and approaches broadly applicable. In the writing I have relied heavily on Ruth Cohn's theme-centered interactional method of group leading. I have found it to be simple, useful, and complete and would invite the reader's study of her theory and technique in her forthcoming book, which is not yet titled. The present, most complete presentations of her ideas appear in *Confrontation* (1972), edited by Leonard Blank et al.

PREPARATION OF THE LEADER

Many professionals were probably trained in leading groups as I was—"by the seat of the pants." When I was preparing to become a psychologist, it was almost sacrilegious and certainly laughable if an individual spent much time preparing to lead a group session. Heavy emphasis was placed on interpersonal dynamics, openness in communication, and on doing what came naturally. I have found, however, that lack of preparation for group leadership is irresponsible and generally indicates either the group leader's unwillingness to undertake the task of preparing for the group or an ignorance of how to go about doing so. Particularly in multiracial and transcultural groups, and in groups made up of inexperienced participants, the leader must provide a format within which the group can interact with a sense of direction.

With this in mind, I would like to mention a number of considerations that I believe a group leader should try to understand before a group begins. Let me make it clear that it is probably impractical to consider every one of these issues. Let me also emphasize that the group leader's understanding before beginning the group can often be in error and may need to be corrected through experience after the group begins. However that does not excuse the leader from making the attempt, and the following factors are highly influential variables in the globe or setting of any live and worthwhile group. It is important to know as much as possible about each before the group convenes.

• Whose idea is it to hold the group? The context and atmosphere of a group in which the idea came from the administration will be significantly different from the one in which the idea of having the group came from the participants themselves.

• Who is coming to the group? The variety of people willing to spend their time in this way can tell the leader much about their expectations and wishes.

• Who is *not* coming and why? Many times key or important people are omitted from group membership either by their own choice or by that of someone else.

- Who is paying for the group and the leadership? The responsibility for or receipt of payment yields either real or imagined power and influence.

- What have the group members been told about the group? Were they forewarned of the group's formation? Were they pressured? Is attendance mandatory? Were the announcements candid or devious?

- Who has the clout? Will persons in the power structure be represented either directly or indirectly within the group? What is their attitude toward holding the group?

- How does the boss or the usual leader of the group feel about you as the leader? Resentment and competitiveness, as well as enthusiasm and anticipation, will have an influence upon the way the leader is seen by the group members.

- What is the best estimate of what the group members suspect and/or expect from the group? Members almost always bring unrealistic positive or negative fantasies to the group based on what they have been told or what they have imagined.

- What is the group's association with others outside the group? How does this group relate to what is going on in the neighborhood or organization? How may these factors influence the group's reaction and/or behavior in the group experience?

- Where is the meeting? Why is it there? What effect might the selection of the site have on the members of the group? The physical setting of a meeting always sets a mood which must be taken into account.

- How can distractions be minimized? There will always be distractions of noise, interruptions, scheduling, emergencies, temperature control, or outside commitments of members which will influence the flow and interaction within the group. Unless a discussion of these distractions is a major purpose of the group, some means of minimizing them is necessary.

- What are the facilities? Are the facilities appropriate to the theme or task of the group? It is as hard for a group of business executives to warm to the task of sitting on the floor and discussing the state of the economy as it is for a group of ghetto residents to warm to the task of meeting in the sterile comfort of a large conference room to discuss crime in the ghetto community.

- What are the folkways, mores, and codes of the group? The leader need not necessarily adhere to the group's standards, but if his or her style of dress, speech, or mannerisms are foreign to the group, the differences will undoubtedly be factors to consider and possibly to discuss within the group.

- What are the big hidden agenda items? What can you find out before the group starts about negative personal dynamics? Who hates whom? Who is about to be fired or asked to leave? Who is snubbed or thought to be stupid or uncooperative? Who feels unappreciated? Who are the known big talkers? In any group where the members know one another, individual members may become trapped in their reputations and find it difficult or impossible to escape these preconceived images held by other group members. If improved communication is one of you goals as a group leader, your planning should include these factors.

The leader will want to keep in mind that the group organizers with whom he or she will be conferring before starting the group probably do not have totally accurate information. They may be blinded in their perceptions by their own biases and prejudices, as well as by inaccurate assessment of individual styles and personality patterns. The leader should listen closely, include their views in the planning, then be prepared to change and/or modify his original ideas and directions. Group leaders should also bear in mind that it is generally much easier to be compassionate, understanding, and open-minded when one does not have to live or work with an individual on a regular basis. The leader need not be blinded by other people's perceptions and projections, but it would be fallacious for him or her to believe that other people's perceptions of their comrades, fellow workers, or family members have no validity.

THE THEME-CENTERED INTERACTIONAL METHOD

THE TRIANGLE WITHIN THE GLOBE.   The theme-centered interactional method (TCI) conceptualizes the group process as having three main elements (the triangle), all contained within the context or frame of reference in which the group functions (the globe). The triangle consists of (1) the task or theme of the group; (2) the "We" factors or interpersonal flow between and among group members; and (3) the "I" factors—the idiosyncratic, unique factors brought to the experience by each individual group member. The globe includes all of the factors, both physical and emotional, that surround and intrude upon the participants in the group. The group leader's tasks are to understand and anticipate as many globe factors as possible; to comprehend the group dynamics so as to formulate a task or theme in a way that conforms to the purposes of the group; and to balance the group interaction between the task or theme, the interpersonal communication factors, and the individual, "I", idiosyncratic factors that preoccupy each member of the group.

THEME SETTING.   A major contribution of the theme-centered interactional method of group leading is its emphasis on the importance of a theme to a group. A theme serves as a general road map describing in broad outline the territory the group is to explore. It includes in its structure and wording the leader's best appraisal of the general direction in which the group is to move. The theme also provides a foundation to which to return when a group becomes stagnated or when it has sufficiently finished one task and seems ready to turn to another. The setting of a theme and the contemplation of it before the group starts talking exert a great influence over the direction and content of a session, often without any conscious recognition by group members that they are attending to the task or the theme at hand.

Group leaders who have not tried the theme-centered approach may find it awkward at first to set an appropriate theme with the group. Leaders may make mistakes in the way that themes are worded, and may occasionally misread the flow and interpersonal relationships already present within a group, attempting to head it in a direction that is completely inappropriate. For example, if feelings of animosity and resentment are running high, a theme such as "caring more for one another" will probably cause the group to bog down completely, for the interpersonal feelings are so strong in the opposite direction that they need to be worked through before caring can take place. A simple change in the theme to "discovering how we avoid caring for one another" or "discovering how I avoid caring for you" will zero in on the problem and be the catalyst for dramatic and growth-producing interaction. Leaders should be willing to experiment with theme setting, for themes can be used in any kind of group meeting. The reader is referred to Mrs. Cohn's article in *Confrontation* (1972) for some specific principles of theme setting.

KINDS OF GROUPS

TASK GROUPS.   Groups can form or be formed for a number of different purposes, and these should be reflected in themes for the group. A task-oriented group might have as its theme teaching English 101, planning a class party, preparing a budget, planning our weekend, assessing our community's needs, deciding on a new building, and the like. In each of these focused themes, the main purpose of the group is reflected in a task that the group has yet to accomplish.

"WE" GROUPS.   A second major type of group is a "We"-oriented group. Themes in such a group are interpersonally oriented and are designed to increase the flow of communication and understanding between and among group members. Examples of this type of theme include sharing our troubles, finding friends, discovering gaps between us, pulling apart-pulling together, overcoming barriers between us, appreciating differences, or sharing our similarities. Here the main focus of the group is on facilitating interpersonal understanding and communication. Generally speaking, these groups considerably decrease any hostility, competitiveness, and misunderstanding among group members.

"I" GROUPS.   A third group is more individual or "I"-oriented. Themes for this group focus primarily upon individual understanding and personal growth. Examples of themes in this type of group would be helping you understand me, sharing my shyness, being a leader of myself, improving my life, looking at me through your eyes, showing you my distrust, opening myself to play, or sharing my goals. Such themes are most appropriate in therapy groups, counseling groups, church or Sunday school groups, rehabilitation groups, personal growth groups, and others in which primary emphasis is upon individual self-understanding, expanding capabilities, and enhancing self-awareness and personal growth.

DISTURBANCES

A group leader must recognize that disturbances and passionate involvements take precedence over whatever else is transpiring in the group. Disturbances can take the form of physical disruptions, such as noise, temperature variations, or other outside environmental factors that make it difficult for individuals within the group to attend to the task at hand. They can also take the form of personal discomforts, such as being hungry, having to urinate badly, or sitting too close to someone who is offensive. Disturbances can also be mental or psychological, such as feeling depressed, feeling worried about or preoccupied with some private concern, feeling intensely angry at someone else in the group, feeling bored, or being unclear about procedures.

A rule of thumb is that any disturbance that makes any group member unable to attend to the task at hand needs to be surfaced and discussed. Often this procedure is all that is needed to take care of the problem, but sometimes the disturbance may be so compelling that it needs more attention. However the disturbance should be dealt with only until the people involved can return to the task or theme. Disturbances can usually be ascertained by watching for signs of physical discomfort, asking the group directly if there is anything that is keeping them from being involved in the theme, and paying attention to side conversations which often contain the essence of what the leader needs to know to understand the group process at that moment. Often a simple go-around—asking each group member to retain what he or she was thinking or feeling when the leader stopped the group process, and restricting each one to a single, simple comment—will allow the leader to pick up disturbances and factors of which the leader was unaware. There is one thing to remember, however: When the leader conducts a go-around, he or she should be prepared for surprises and considerable individual differences in the kinds of comments and degrees of involvement. Even though individuals have been trained to ignore disturbances, the fact is that disturbances usually supersede and interfere with any but the most dramatic and involved tasks.

GROUP THEMES AND TECHNIQUES

In many transcultural groups the primary goal or target is increased feelings of "groupness" or "We-ness." This group feeling can only be accomplished through increased sharing, increased communication, and increased understanding between and among group members. Listed below are several themes and procedures that are particularly useful in working toward increased feelings of "We-ness" and that help to enhance understanding, openness, and sharing.

Recently I conducted a group whose 11 members were the professional staff in a public school system. A great deal of antagonism, alienation, and poor communication was reported to exist among the various staff members. In addition, a recent budget cut would soon necessitate the removal of three of them (yet to be announced). The workshop was planned for just one-half day, and one of my tasks as the group's leader was to promote increased interpersonal understanding, cooperation, and communication.

First I made a brief introductory comment, focusing on my feelings of being overawed with the responsibility of conducting this workshop with a group that appeared to be under so much stress. I then suggested "looking at me through your eyes" as a theme for our first session. I asked the group to pair off with spaces between the pairs throughout the fairly large room in which we were meeting. I then asked them to spend 2 minutes in silence, deciding what they believed the other person saw in them and believed them to be. When this period was over, I asked one of them to volunteer to share with his partner what he or she believed the other person saw in him or her. The recipient was simply to listen. At the end of the first sharing, the roles were switched and the individual who had been listening shared with his/her partner what he or she believed the other person thought him to be. Following the second period of sharing, time was left for the couple to interact.

This is an example of a theme that seemed to be exactly right for the group at that moment and worked exceedingly well to focus on projections and imaginary images in quite a helpful way. When we gathered back together, the feeling of "We-ness" in the group had grown considerably, and sharing was much easier than it had been before, although none of the reality problems had changed.

Because transcultural groups often evidence suspicion, fear, misunderstanding, and efforts at personal and emotional survival, a theme like "sharing suspicions" sometimes gets the interpersonal ball rolling quickly. When such a theme is used, after a period of silence to allow people to get in touch with their feelings and suspicions, the leader can start off by sharing his or her suspicions in as honest and straightforward a manner as possible, without being accusatory, attacking, or devastating to group members. It must be remembered that the leader's opinion is usually more highly regarded than any other group member's, and the leader has some responsibility for being selectively authentic—certainly much more so than any other group member. Even if the leader suspects that one of the members is being consciously and maliciously belittling or humiliating of another or is being a "phony friend," it may not be helpful or wise to share those perceptions in just those terms. One may be honest without saying all he knows or all he suspects, but a group leader's willingness to share some of these suspicions, whether they be right or wrong, will generally encourage others to be honest and open about their own feelings.

In all but the briefest groups, there comes a time when negative feelings have accumulated to the point where they become inhibitive and a stumbling block for the group. The negative feelings can represent the range of human experience, because some people find feelings of love, sex, and joy just as negative as feelings of hostility, jealousy, resentment, envy, or sadness. Often when a group seems stagnated and vibrations of negative feelings and animosity are clearly evident, a session should and can be devoted to dealing with negative feelings.

This is a theme that many group leaders avoid. However I have consistently found it a theme which, by encouraging expression within the group context of these important feelings, moves the group toward increased understanding and communication. Working with this theme usually uncovers a variety of feelings (many of which the group leader was unaware [of]) which may include a liberal mixture of projection, bitchiness, impatience, and boredom, and many messages that imply that in TA terms, "You're not OK." The airing of such feelings with the opportunity for feedback is an essential step in any group relationship. Unverbalized and unexpressed negative feelings always constitute a powerful hidden agenda, and no group that has the purpose of becoming a well-functioning interpersonal, communicative group can achieve its goal without working through these inevitable feelings of negativism.

One activity that helps people become aware of other people's impressions of them is called "sharing my impressions." The group breaks itself down into units of no more than four to six people. Within each small group, individuals use pencil and paper to share various types of impressions, depending upon the purpose of the group. The reactive questions can vary. "What is your impression of each group member?" "What was your first impression of each?" "What is your impression of how each would serve as a leader if this group were involved in a task?" "How do you feel you might encounter difficulty with this person as a leader?" "What would be your impression of this person as a mother? . . . as a child? . . . as a business companion?" After a silent period while impressions are being written, group members can either read their impressions aloud, or they can give all impressions of individual A to individual A, of individual B to individual B, and so on. Individuals may then share these impressions aloud, depending on the condition of the group leader's desire either to increase or decrease stress and open sharing within the group. Impressions given this way almost always provide food for thought; and although group members' pictures of themselves are often jolted, seldom does this technique become a disruptive influence. This technique would have been totally inappropriate, however, for the group mentioned earlier in which I used the "looking at me through your eyes," for the hostility and the mutual mistrust were already so pervasive in that group that open negative comments would have simply fed the fire.

Almost always a feeling of "We-ness" or "groupness" will be enhanced or developed if a group building technique is used. A theme like "exploring what I've always wanted to know about you and never dared ask" is inappropriate for a large group, but it can facilitate the building of "We-ness" when only two people are involved in a face-to-face situation. For example, if interpersonal communication is the major concern in a group and if a feeling of "We-ness" seems to be lacking, an excellent technique is to break the large group into dyads and to let the two individuals pursue a theme like the one stated above for 10 to 30 minutes. At the end of that time, each group of two chooses another group of two to become a group of four using the same theme. When all members gather together in the last part of the session, they will ordinarily experience a period of stiffness following the intimate sharing that has occurred in the dyads and the quartets. At this point the leader can help reduce this feeling of inhibition by asking individuals to reflect on how they feel about coming back to the larger group. Sharing these feelings brings the small groups together and helps promote "We-ness" in the large group. This technique is much superior to asking for a report of the experience in the small group, for that usually turns into a dead rehash rather than a lively, present-minute situation.

In every group, but particularly in transcultural groups, there are individuals who feel as though they have a lot to offer and there are others who feel they have little to offer. One very useful theme for dealing with this situation is "teaching you—letting you teach me." A group of six to eight members is ideal for this exercise. Each individual is given a slip of paper for each other group member. On one side of the paper the individual lists a few things that he or she would like to teach each other group member. Members do not actually have to know how to teach what they list. The number of items listed for each group member will vary considerably, but whatever the person chooses to list is sufficient. After this task is completed, individuals are asked to turn the pages over and to list on the other side what they would like to learn from each group member. At the conclusion of the exercise each individual in the group has a slip of paper for every group member, indicating the things he or she would like to teach each other person, and on the other side, the things he or she would like to learn from the other. Next, individuals volunteer to have the group share aloud what the group would like to teach them. Or individuals volunteer to call upon the group members from whom they would like to hear. Then individuals share what they would like other group members to teach them. This exercise is excellent for increasing interpersonal understanding and communication and for giving individuals a view of themselves from the outside. It is best done after the group has met for a few sessions and individuals have had a chance to learn about each other, and it should always be followed with an opportunity for discussion, review, and feedback to allow expression of the feelings that were generated during such an interaction.

THE SOCIAL THERMOMETER.   This technique allows group members to express differing attitudes and shades of viewpoints on any topic. It can be used in a group of any size, 6 to 10 participants being an ideal number. Larger groups can select or self-select group members to participate, with the exact number dependent upon such factors as the amount of time available. The group leader formulates a statement such as, "I believe taxes should be increased," "I believe this group is a waste of time," or "I believe women need more love than men." The participants usually want to clarify the statement in some way or to make it more explicit, but the leader asks them simply to think it over and decide how they feel or think about that particular statement. They are then asked to arrange themselves along an imaginary line drawn down the middle of the room with total agreement represented at one end, total disagreement represented at the other end, and a neutral position in the middle. All participants then move simultaneously to the point which represents the degree to which they agree or disagree with the statement. Once every member is standing in his or her position, they may ask only one question, "Why are you standing where you are?" The person answers, but no debate or argument is allowed.

Following the questioning of as many members as is feasible, those standing are allowed to change positions if they wish as a result of new information that they have acquired during the questioning period. The audience and the group are then allowed another round of asking and responding to the question, "Why do you stand where you do?" In my experience this technique has never failed to provide for the sharing of varied points of view in an acceptable, nonthreatening context that leads to free discussion and increased understanding among group members.

OPENING UP THE GROUP'S PRIVATE WORLD

In transcultural groups, as in most groups, members may be reluctant to participate freely and openly. Most of us have grown up with the belief that if we have a problem, we should solve it ourselves rather than seek outside help or counsel. This belief is common in many cultures. Individuals have learned that they should keep family problems at home and should not talk to strangers about them or share them with people outside the immediate family structure. This belief is rooted so deeply in many people that it causes them to feel like traitors if they discuss any problems or concerns with outsiders, and they feel particularly inhibited if the outsiders come from other cultural groups.

Equally common is the belief of many persons that if other people knew what they really thought or how they really felt, the other people would think less of them, would dislike them, would not associate with them, or would think them crazy or unusual or strange. The group leader's opinion is usually regarded as particularly important, and group members will sometimes go to great lengths to keep the group leader from ascertaining their faults, embarrassing habits, perceived weaknesses, or personal fears and doubts, as well as their life problems. It is also very common to find individuals who will talk very freely about their problems or opinions at the hairdresser's or with the bartender, but who are reluctant to talk about them in any group setting where a designated leader is seen as a professional or an expert.

These feelings of resistance and reluctance to share, particularly when the group's purpose is to promote "We-ness" or to share "I" feelings, must be dealt with in some manner. In any ongoing group a theme needs to be designed to focus directly upon individual and group resistance and to encourage a more open exchange of forbidden topics or ideas. Examples of such themes would be sharing impressions, sharing a few of my personal secrets, finding what keeps me from saying what I think (or feel), remembering people I can share with.

DEALING WITH PATRONIZING HELPERS

One of the most common, early problems in a group is the group member who conveys the attitude that he or she is the knowledgeable one, there to share ideas, directions, and brilliance with the less fortunate group members. Too often the person who acts this way is the group's designated leader. Such leadership usually breaks the group into two main segments—those who are impressed, agreeable and generally silent, and those who are unimpressed, angered, threatened, and silent. Common symptoms of this particular attitude are conveyed in the general impression this person gives of "having the solution," or in such statements as, "I used to be that way until . . . " "You're not acting right," "Look what works for me," or "Let me tell you how to do it." The group leader who notices such attitudes in subtle and not-so-subtle forms coming from a group member, or even from himself, can usually expedite a feeling of "We-ness" in the group by simply asking the group members to express their response to what the rather insensitive "helper" has just said. It is less dramatic, but equally effective, to ask the member who has just expounded on his philosophy to life—leaving the definite impression that he or she has the answer to any problem—"How did what you just said sound to you?" or "How do you believe the other group members are responding to what you said?"

THE IMPASSE

In every group's evolution there comes a time when the mood of the group is down, when people are thinking of leaving, when there are feelings of awkwardness, superficiality, or uneasiness and the group seems to be on the verge of collapse. This stage usually occurs after several sessions have been held. It can be delayed and partially avoided by filling the group's time with enough activities to keep the members occupied and entertained; but sooner or later, the group, both individually and collectively, needs to face its discomfort or it will indeed continue to deteriorate. It is here that the group leader's skill and experience come into play most strikingly.

Groups vary in the degree to which this problem can be confronted directly, but most groups are salvaged and enlivened if the group leader focuses upon how the various group members feel about being in that group at that moment, whether the group has met their expectations, what they are disappointed in, and how they can go about achieving for themselves what they wish to achieve in the group. Usually initiating another activity or being too forceful will simply aggravate the feelings and increase the likelihood that the group will disintegrate. It is at this time that the group leader must be firm in his commitment to group process, be willing to examine where he may have erred in overlooking important factors (particularly negative feelings) within the group, but know that the group can work through this stage to become even stronger and more cohesive.

This situation is analagous to making one's way in a sailboat from one point to another. In any sailing venture there are going to be wind shifts, some of which can be anticipated and some of which cannot. When a sudden shift of wind brings a boat to a standstill, the captain must then exercise sufficient knowledge, patience, and skill to get his boat moving again. Such is the way of the group leader. Although sailing and group leading are skills which can be taught, truly exceptional group leaders develop the same keen sense of timing and technique that also separates great sailors from merely good ones.

GROUP DECISION MAKING

I am consistently fascinated at the effectiveness of a group in which there are good interpersonal communication, free expression of ideas and feelings, and a relative absence of hidden agendas. For example, when I served as the director of a fairly large community guidance clinic, word was received that overall salary increases could not exceed 5% of the total salary budget for the preceding year. Anticipating a long and difficult struggle, but having just returned from a workshop with a great deal of enthusiasm, I suggested that the various program leaders within the guidance clinic meet with me and that together we decide on salary levels for all employees, including ourselves. The only guideline established was that salary levels could not exceed the 5% limit. My suggestion met with a good bit of skepticism. This plan may have taken somewhat more time, but I found that many significant items were brought up, discussed, and integrated into the overall budget plan. In the long run I believe this procedure saved time. Each program leader was knowledgeable about and had helped determine the final figures, and each was able to explain the new salaries in detail to his or her own staff. It was surprising how much unanimity there was about most staff positions. In retrospect my only regret is that more of the junior staff was not involved in the sessions. The only complaints and hard feelings came from those who were not included in the decision-making process.

GROUP DISTANCE AND COMMUNICATION FLOW

Leaders and groups can be arranged and conceptualized in many ways, according to the distances and dimensions of both psychological and physical space. One of the most common arrangements is for the leader to be removed from the group as in most classrooms. In this arrangement communications flow primarily from the leader to the group, with only occasional input from a group member to the leader. Such groups are usually task-oriented and generally lack the component of "We-ness" or group cohesiveness, except as those feelings are generated in support of or in opposition to the leader's view. A dead learning situation like this can be changed to a living learning situation in several ways: by rearranging the members physically to minimize the distance between the leader and the group members; by the leader's recognition that most people cannot listen to a leader for more than 2 or 3 minutes at a time; by providing an opportunity for regular and/or spontaneous interchange among the group and between the group and its leader; by proper theme setting and introduction; and by occasionally attending to "We and I" concerns within the group.

Another group concept places the leader in the center of a circle of group members. This type of group is also leader-oriented, with communications flowing primarily between individuals and the leader. In this situation it is likely that a large number of individual viewpoints and concerns will be expressed, but that very little feeling of "We-ness" or group cohesiveness will evolve. Very possibly the leader is taking on too much responsibility and is not trusting the group members to assume responsibility for themselves. To promote group feeling, the leader usually needs only to recognize that individuals within the group have much to offer each other and to suggest that individuals speak to other group members as well as to the leader. Adapting the flow of communication in this manner will increase feelings of group cohesiveness.

A third picture is a circle of individuals, with communication apparently flowing at random back and forth between all of the various members of the group. In such a group all members are involved to the extent they wish to be, individual and group concerns are dealt with openly, and the members generally develop a strong group feeling. Generally speaking, the leader participates as a group member whose additional main concerns are to attend to disturbances that seem to impede the flow of the group and occasionally to bring the group back to the task or theme if it goes too far afield.

COMMON ERRORS MADE BY GROUP LEADERS

Some group leaders assume that to be effective they must remain aloof and assume the role of a sage or authority in order to help people progress toward the goal that has been set. Such removal of one's self from the group process alienates, aggravates, and causes suspicion among the group members and is completely unnecessary. Group members generally feel much more capable of sharing if the group leader also shares of himself. Aloofness is generally a mask for feelings of incompetency or boredom, either of which, if unrecognized, cripples group functioning.

In an effort to facilitate communication and good feelings, some leaders will do their utmost to become a buddy or a companion to the group members. Generally speaking, it takes group members a long time to be able to accept the person in authority as an equal, and this acceptance is generally accomplished by the leader's showing humanness and foibles as well as knowledge and experience. Only in this way can the leader be experienced by the group as a person and a comrade. Nothing falls flatter than a middle-aged group leader, raised in a conservative tradition, trying to relate as an equal or a compatriot to a group of teenagers, particularly when the youths are from a different cultural background. They know and the leader knows that there are giant gaps in experience and understanding; and it is much more useful to recognize, understand, and appreciate the gaps than to try to bridge them by artificial means.

Group leaders do not necessarily have to have a thorough knowledge of the task at hand in a task-oriented group in order to lead the group effectively. True, it might be ideal if the group leader could have a broad store of information about the task as well as skills in group leading and the processes of group interaction. It is, however, entirely possible for an individual to lead a group on "planning our next semester" or "planning our budget" when the group leader has minimal knowledge of either curriculum design or finance. The leader can see to it that the flow of communication is facilitated and that a balance is maintained between the task and the "We and I" forces during the course of the group meeting. Group leading is not the same as judging, and a group leader can effectively ensure that a variety of viewpoints are expressed and considered so that the final result of the group's efforts represents the wishes of the majority.

A major mistake is to allow a group to believe that what they need to solve their problems or what they need to complete the group process is not available to them in the present situation. It is extremely disruptive to a group to focus upon materials, people, or factors outside the group situation or meeting room. When group members are encouraged to make use of the materials at hand and use their imaginations, amazing things can happen. If some important person is not present, rather than spend a lot of time speculating about how things would be different if that person were there, it is much more productive to have some individual assume the role of that person, playing the part as authentically as possible. The human imagination and human emotional functioning are the most valuable tools of any group process, and reliance on and use of them will usually lead to deeper understanding.

In many of our workshops, for example, we have a theme called "opening myself to play." The procedure is for individuals to recall games they played in childhood and to pick a game that seems for any reason to be important to them. After all the games have been reported to the group, the leader suggests to the group members that we play as many of these games as possible. Members always protest that it is impossible to play the games because the proper equipment is not there or the environment is wrong; but once the group becomes excited about using the resources of the room to duplicate what already exists only in fantasy, these sessions often become beautiful, poignant, and meaningful experiences. Undoubtedly, one can find exceptions to this principle of using immediate resources and situation. However every group believes that its situation is the exception, and exceptions are much more rare than are applications of the rule.

HELPFUL HINTS FOR LEADERS

Insist, insofar as possible, that individuals within the group refer to themselves in the first person. Culturally we are accustomed to speaking of "you" and "they." Communications will be enhanced if members use the terms "I" and "We."

Ask that any speaker address directly the person to whom he or she is speaking. Too often group members speak of people sitting next to them in the third person, as if they were not in the room.

Keep as much of the discussion as possible related to the here and now of the group. Questions like, "Can you see how that relates here?" "Who here seems to remind you of that?" or "Who have you seen here that acts that way?" are questions that keep the focus within the group and keep the interaction relevant and involving.

Set a time for beginning and ending the group, and work toward that end. Occasional reminders of the amount of time remaining are extremely helpful, and the group will function more efficiently if it is aware that it must end on time. There will be occasions when groups can profitably continue past the closing time, but if that is the rule rather than the exception, your group is not doing what it should be doing during the time allotted. An hour and a half is usually a good length of time for group sessions. If the group seems unready for closure, a simple question like, "How do you feel about continuing the group or finishing now?" or "How much time do you feel we should allot to finish this?" will usually provide the leader with all the information he or she needs to make the decision.

Encourage members to speak one at a time. A group can attend to only one discussion at a time, and the group leader may often find it necessary to insist on this rule. Deciding who should continue should ordinarily not be the leader's decision. Within reason, the leader should call side conversations into focus, encouraging the individuals who are engaging in the side conversations to share their thoughts with the group. This procedure is not intended to embarrass the individuals but is based on the observation that often side conversations contain thoughts or feelings that need to be brought out and reacted to by other group members.

Actively discourage individuals from speaking for someone else and encourage individuals to speak for themselves. Too often a member will say, "Jane had her feelings hurt by what you said," or "You shouldn't talk like that in front of Jane." Unless the group leader calls attention to the fact that Jane is not speaking for herself, many times interpretations will be compounded to the point of chaos.

After writing the substance of this chapter and before formulating its conclusion, I traveled to another state to help lead a week-long intensive group in which the task was to teach the participants group-leading skills as well as to provide a meaningful interpersonal experience for them. Represented in the group were Germans, Italians, a Turk, several Orthodox Jews, southern Protestants, northeastern liberals, psychiatrists, social workers, housewives, and a labor union organizer. Group members ranged in age from 17 to 60. There were people whose external beauty was considerable and those whose beauty was essentially internal. They also differed in experience, background, values, attitudes, life style, and any number of characteristics. By following the techniques and using many of the themes which have been described here, however, the group was able to work its way to one of the greatest, most intensive experiences in which I have ever participated. That is saying quite a bit, because I have participated in many. The techniques and ideas outlined in this chapter have been shown over and over again to be useful with many kinds of groups and are especially effective when barriers of ethnic or cultural differences inhibit communication and understanding. It takes great patience and practice to integrate the above ideas and techniques into one's own leadership style, but the rewards are great and worth all the effort to acquire them.

References

Cohn, R. C. Living-learning encounters: The theme-centered interactional method. In L. Blank, et al. (Eds.), *Confrontation: Encounters in self and interpersonal awareness.* New York: Macmillan, 1972, pp. 245–273.

Cohn, R. C. *Living-learning encounters: The theme-centered interactional method.* (Mimeograph) 1969.

Cohn, R. C. Style and spirit of theme-centered interactional method. In S. Kaplan and C. Sager (Eds.), *Progress in group and family therapy.* New York: Brunner Mazel, 1972, pp. 852–878.

Gazda, G. M. *Group counseling.* Boston: Allyn & Bacon, 1972.

Gordon, M. *Theme-centered interaction: An original focus on counseling and education.* Baltimore: National Educational Press, Inc., 1972.

Chapter 6

CROSS-CULTURAL GROUP COUNSELING AND ITS EFFECT ON REDUCING TENSION IN A RACIALLY MIXED SCHOOL

Richard Strub

The need to reduce tensions between black and white students in a recently desegregated school caused counselors to get involved. This chapter describes how cross-cultural group counseling had a positive effect in helping students move from vocal and physical confrontation to dialogue and discussion as a way of resolving problems. Evaluation of the groups was undertaken, and copies of questionnaires administered to students and faculty and administrators are included in the appendices, together with samples of actual comments made by each group.

In recent years the civil rights movement has encouraged efforts to improve school programs and to enrich the learning environment for all students. The attention given to integration and desegregation of schools has resulted in attempts to develop strategies to increase the potential educational benefits to all individuals. Many of these attempts have either failed or have been only minimally successful. Bringing about change in the schools is more difficult than might be anticipated.

In the late 1960s the University of Northern Iowa, like innumerable other institutions, became increasingly concerned about the need for better racial understandings among the students. In responding to this need, the University wished to participate actively in seeking solutions rather than to assume a compassionate albeit apathetic stance.

While the university community was attempting to make overall constructive changes, attention became specifically focused on the virtually all-white university laboratory school where it was decided to try to change the racial composition of the student body. Since the community of Cedar Falls had only a small number of black residents, it was necessary to enlist the cooperation of the Waterloo Community School Board and volunteer black families residing in that nearby city. With this cooperation secured, a bussing program began in September of 1968.

The first year of the program passed without incident. As the number of black students increased and the novelty of their presence in the school wore off, however, increasing tensions during the second and third year demonstrated that the period of calm was over. Racial interactions were accomplished only with friction, between black students and white students as well as between black students and white teachers. Racial and ethnic slurs appeared on walls and other places throughout the building. Verbal accusations concerning the honesty of black students were expressed by a small vocal group. Black students claimed that they were excluded from some student-elected activities, especially cheerleading and student government.

Within the school it was apparent that blacks and whites were becoming polarized. Previously ignored or submerged questions regarding the wisdom of the project were now finding their way to the surface. It was obvious that the bussing of a minority from one community to another could not, in and of itself, accomplish the goal of increased racial understanding in the receiving community. Apparent, too, was the fact that bussing was creating some unanticipated negative side effects for black students. Bussing limited their participation in after-school activities, and although it did give them the chance to discuss their problems and enabled them to cope better with a hostile environment, it proved counterproductive to the establishment of improved black-white interactions.

Noting the deteriorating trends in actions and attitudes, school officials began to discuss possible solutions to the problems. Effective solutions were not easily found, and no real progress was made. As so often happens, the leisurely pace toward a solution was interrupted by a confrontation between a black high school boy and a white boy. During the scuffle, the white student received a knife wound. The reaction to this incident held the potential for imminent group violence. At this point school personnel determined that formal intervention was necessary.

USE OF COUNSELING GROUPS

Because the black students had often discussed their frustrations with the school counselors, the decision was made to experiment with group counseling as a means to a calmer climate. Three counseling groups were formed— one senior high group and two junior high groups. Initially the groups were made up entirely of black students. This was not because it was believed that they were the primary instigators of the problems; rather it was because their grievances seemed more immediate and compelling. The sessions were facilitated primarily by a black counselor, with a white counselor providing limited assistance. These early groups were primarily cathartic in nature and were intended to defuse the potentially explosive situation. They were formed to give the black students some assurance that they had an opportunity to express their grievances and frustrations. The result was what appeared to be a slightly more relaxed attitude on their part.

Although the catharsis that took place in these sessions was valuable, the black students in the high school group realized that they alone could not reduce the racial disharmony in the school. If the groups were to achieve this goal, they needed to include influential white students. Therefore black students identified several white students who were not only influential but who also on occasion had demonstrated negative behavior toward black students and had been participants in some racial conflicts. Not knowing exactly what would happen, and with some apprehension, the counselors and the secondary school principal invited the white students who had been identified by the black students to participate in the group sessions. With very few exceptions, they agreed to do so. This, then, was the beginning of cross-cultural counseling groups.

The original senior high group consisted of eight black students and eight white students in grades 10, 11, and 12. Within 1 week after the newly formed senior high group had its first session, the black junior high groups asked also to become biracial. One of these groups was formed in the same way as the senior high group, by including white junior high students deemed by black students to be influential and to have exhibited negative behavior toward them. The second junior high group was formed differently. Many white students in the school expressed the desire to make a positive contribution toward improving relationships between black and white students and volunteered to be involved in the cross-cultural discussions. Therefore this second junior high group consisted of eight black students and eight white students who had asked to be involved.

The adult facilitators of the high school group were a black male counselor, a white male counselor, and a black male social studies instructor who was studying for an advanced degree in counseling. Sessions were usually held once a week and lasted approximately 1 hour. Occasionally 2-hour sessions were conducted when the students felt they were necessary.

In initial sessions the counselors pointed out the tremendous potential that the group sessions had for effecting change in the emotional climate in the school. Several basic ground rules that would contribute to a successful group experience were proposed and adopted by the participants. Some of these were:

1. We cannot help each other if we refuse to be honest. Let's try not to let our previous ideas get in our way.
2. Try to really listen to what the other person is saying. Don't just try to convince him or her that you are right. Listen to what he or she says, just as you expect him or her to listen to you when you have something to say.
3. One of the best ways you can help others is to let them know that they are not alone in what they feel. If you have experienced the same feelings, tell them. You may be surprised to find that you will be able to understand more about the way you feel as you find yourself talking to others about how they feel.
4. Do not feel that you have to come to a group solution or agreement. The purpose of the group is to explore topics together and to reach better understandings.

The students were quite guarded and defensive in their comments in the early sessions. It was apparent to the counselors that an atmosphere of warmth, calm, and acceptance would encourage open communication. The techniques used were not unlike those used in typical monoracial confrontation sessions. However, although the counselors were not entirely aware of it at the time, the interactions and positive behavior of the black and white counselors served to model the importance of dialogue and discussion in building trust, respect, and acceptance among and between people of different races.

As time elapsed and the students felt less threatened, they began to communicate more openly and to deal with such considerations as: (1) reasons why the blacks came to the laboratory school; (2) feelings of whites regarding Waterloo blacks in the school; (3) circumstances leading to the knifing incident; (4) parental attitudes about integration; (5) black students' rejection of white students' attempts to be friendly; and (6) reasons for an unwillingness on both sides to make friendships.

The junior high groups tended not to be as confrontation-oriented in these early stages as were the older students. While they expressed their feelings and questioned each other, the younger students demonstrated more openness and tended to show less hostility toward members of the other racial group. Discussions on various topics were more superficial and less in-depth than those experienced by the older students.

As the sessions continued throughout the year, black students expressed their sensitivities about things white students either intentionally or unintentionally were doing and saying. White students in turn voiced their feelings about actions of black students that angered them. Discussion also centered on potentially explosive terms like *boy, nigger, honkey, jungle bunny,* and *you people.*

The terms *Uncle Tom* and *oreo* were examined, with considerable discussion of their meaning and implications in the school setting. This led to some clarification of why there was an unwillingness on both sides, particularly on the part of the more militant students, to make friendships. Black students did not want to be called *Toms,* and white students did not want to be called *nigger-lovers.*

Near the end of the first year and into the second year of the cross-cultural counseling groups, the students began to be able to discuss topics that were not so fraught with emotion. Among these were the need for more black faculty members; the desirability of the school's having a larger percentage of black students; problems related to transportation (e.g., the difficulties involved in participation by the black students in after-school activities, and in getting back to Cedar Falls for night activities either as participants or spectators after they had returned to their Waterloo homes at the end of the school day); the difficulty of making friends with individuals whose homes were in another town; and interracial dating and marriage. In those groups where a majority of the white students had some degree of empathy with the difficulties black students had encountered, there were often discussions about the racist attitudes and actions of society in general and some students in particular.

An additional development during the second and third years of the counseling groups was the students' request to focus sometimes on discussions unrelated to race. They began to examine their concerns relative to the possibility of the laboratory school's being closed by the Iowa State Board of Regents; a visit by a legislative budget committee; faculty behaviors and attitudes; school regulations; opportunities for the students during their free periods; and the potential that the cross-cultural groups had for effecting change in the school.

In more recent years the counselors have introduced values clarification strategies to the junior high cross-cultural discussion groups and to an ongoing racially mixed volunteer group of eleventh and twelfth graders. These students were from an independent study class and decided to form the group after hearing a discussion concerning the nature of values clarification.

In these sessions the students were encouraged to take a personal stand on values-centered concerns. Several of the individual strategies dealt with attitudes about relationships with others—some specifically about racially different people. Some examples of these were

How many of you . . .

——have a close friend of another race?
——would invite a friend of another race to your house?
——are apt to go out of your way to have a family of another race as a neighbor?
——think you are racially prejudiced?
——would attend a predominantly black college?
——would attend a predominantly white college?

After the individuals reacted privately, they were encouraged to comment on their responses if they felt comfortable doing so. These rather structured exercises not only encouraged self-awareness but also helped students explore their feelings and attitudes by having the opportunity to interact with peers.

Throughout this 3-year period, another form of biracial group met occasionally. This could best be described as a direct confrontation group. An incident in the hall, in a classroom, or during the noon hour might trigger a conflict between individuals or small groups of white and black students. Emotions would be extremely high, and verbal attacks and threats were common. The confrontation group would be formed of those individuals most directly involved and usually three or four other individuals who had a more objective view of the situation and were vitally interested in the matter. These sessions often lasted 2 or more hours and usually approached some degree of resolution of the problem before terminating.

An outgrowth of this type of session and the cross-cultural groups in general came about in the autumn of 1972. When senior high students were offered the opportunity to be in the regularly scheduled cross-cultural groups, approximately 20 chose to do so. Of this number, only three were black. During this time relationships in the school appeared to be going quite well, and there was a feeling that the groups were not necessary. Therefore the counselors did not attach too much importance to holding the first session early in the school year.

Shortly afterwards, however, an incident in the hall between a black girl and a white girl threatened to cause serious repercussions throughout the school. Disturbed by these developments, two black students suggested that the students involved in the conflict and those most closely affected by its outcome should discuss the situation and attempt to resolve the disagreements. In an effort to accomplish this task, they, along with the student council president, initiated a group meeting.

The students felt that it was their responsibility to arrive at a solution to this conflict and requested that no faculty members be present. On their own, they were able to solve the problem. Later, on other occasions when conflicts arose, the students began to rely upon dialogue as a means to resolve disagreements. In some of these situations they worked out the difficulties by themselves, while at other times they asked the counselors or the principal for assistance.

It is perhaps important to emphasize again that the strategies, techniques, or counseling approaches used by the counselors in the cross-cultural setting were not as important as the fact that the students felt that adults in the school were aware of and responsive to their difficulties. Students could see that faculty were concerned about the tension and unrest and that they were making a sincere effort to improve the situation. Dialogue and discussion became acceptable substitutes for physical and verbal attack. Although there was no well-defined, easily identifiable turning point in the relationships between black and white students in the school, the climate in the school continued to improve. Cross-cultural group counseling does not deserve all of the credit for this change in feelings of mutual acceptance. Time, as well as the efforts of concerned parents, teachers, administrators, and especially students themselves, had much to do with it.

EVALUATION OF EFFECTS OF GROUP COUNSELING

An attempt was made to evaluate the effects and impact of cross-cultural group counseling on reducing tension in the racially-mixed laboratory school by assessing the reactions of three groups of persons. These three groups were the student participants, the teaching faculty, and the school administrators.

The instrument used was a questionnaire developed by the cofacilitators to be administered to participating students (see Appendix A). Selected items from this student questionnaire were also administered to the junior and senior high faculty and administration (see Appendix B).

Findings

The administrators responded more positively than either faculty or students when asked about the effect of the cross-cultural discussion groups on racial harmony. All respondents in this group indicated that without the group discussions, the degree of racial harmony would not have been achieved and, in fact, would have deteriorated. All administrators felt that the discussion groups had, at the minimum, "some positive effect."

The faculty was less positive than administrators but slightly more positive in its responses than the student group. Seventy-seven percent of the faculty and 71% of the students indicated that the discussion groups had "some positive effect" on bringing about racial harmony and understanding in the school. In an item designed to elaborate this facet of the study, 46% of the faculty and 14% of the student participants indicated that without the cross-cultural discussion groups, racial harmony would have lessened.

Seventy-five percent of the administrators indicated that the discussion groups offered a "good opportunity" and 25% felt that they offered "some opportunity" for resolving differences between racial groups by dialogue and discussion. All of this same group felt that the discussions played a useful part in a multiracial school and that groups should continue in following years.

Ninety-five percent of the faculty indicated that the cross-cultural groups offered "some" to "good" opportunity for resolving differences. Eighty-six percent of the faculty and 76% of the students felt that discussion groups played a useful part in a multiracial school. Approximately 95% of the student group indicated that cross-cultural groups should continue in the future, and 86% stated that they would like to participate again. No member of any group indicated that cross-cultural groups should be abandoned in future years.

When questioned about the degree of openness and honesty of communication between black and white students after cross-cultural group counseling, 67% of the student group indicated that students were able to be "moderately" to "very" open and honest in their expressions. Eighty-six percent felt that they themselves were "moderately" to "very" open and honest in their communication.

When student respondents were asked to judge the openness of communication of members of the other racial group, both white and black students indicated that the other racial group exhibited more "holding back" and "faking" of real feelings than did their own. Thirty-eight percent of the black students felt that whites "held back," while only 4% stated that their own racial group tended to do so. Nineteen percent of the whites felt that blacks "held back," while 7% stated that their own racial group acted in this manner.

Although they had no first-hand opportunity to judge the frankness of the dialogue among the students in the group discussions, all of the administrators and 82% of the faculty indicated that the cross-cultural discussion groups had from "some positive effect" to a "strong positive effect" on communication between black and white students. No member of these two groups indicated that any negative effect had occurred in communication between black and white students.

Student attitudes toward racially different students after cross-cultural group counseling were judged to be more positive by administrator and faculty groups than by the student group. All of the administrators and 59% of the faculty indicated that they noticed "more tolerant" student attitudes after the discussion or counseling sessions than they had previously observed. Twenty-seven percent of the faculty thought that the attitudes were "about the same" after the discussions had taken place. Only 28% of the students felt that they were "more tolerant" of students who were racially different from themselves after involvement in the cross-cultural group discussions. Fifty-two percent felt that their attitudes were "about the same," and 10% indicated that they felt "less tolerant" after being involved in the groups.

All of the administrators felt that cross-cultural discussion groups had had "some positive effect" on the attitudes of those students who did not participate. Fifty-nine percent of the faculty felt that there had been "some positive effect" on all students in the school, while 36% indicated that there had been "no effect." No member of these two

a physical confrontation. He had indicated from the beginning that he felt the group discussions were valuable, but that until he matured he could not actively participate and contribute in a positive way.

• Cross-cultural group counseling allowed both black and white students to express some of the emotional feelings and anxieties they had about racial issues. After listening to others communicate their frustrations and concerns in the group sessions, individuals were often relieved and reassured to find out they were not alone in their feelings. Thus they became able to examine their own concerns more realistically and objectively.

• After being involved in discussions for 2 years, senior high black students appeared to be more interested in meeting with students who had the potential to effect direct change in school social interactions. They preferred this to meeting regularly with persons who had volunteered for discussion groups for altruistic purposes. Black students wanted to deal with individuals who could achieve solutions to problems rather than simply engage in intellectual discussions on race relationships.

• Many students who were not directly involved in the groups expressed a desire to join. Others expressed the feeling that it was good that something was being tried, even though they did not care to be involved.

• It is not possible to assess accurately the contributions that the group discussions have had on student behavior, but some general observations of faculty and administrators are listed below: (1) more black students became engaged in extracurricular activities, e.g., music, drama, speech contests, athletics, cheerleading, pep club; (2) a more relaxed atmosphere prevailed throughout the school; (3) blacks were elected to the student council; (4) blacks and whites jointly worked on a plan for a student center; (5) joint planning for an all-school dance resulted in the utilization of a black musical group; and (6) black students appeared to feel that they could express their grievances.

Appendixes C and D contain comments made by students and faculty in response to selected items from the questionnaire.

IMPLICATIONS FOR USE IN OTHER SCHOOLS

Local community attitudes, quality of personnel, administrative openness to confrontation, and other factors would influence the effects this kind of program might have in other settings. However school systems experiencing tensions between racial groups might like to consider the results of this program as they attempt to develop strategies for improving race relations in their own settings.

Listed below are some recommendations for program developers if they wish to implement such a program:

• Student involvement in the discussion groups should be voluntary.

• Time limits on the sessions should be as flexible as possible, particularly if the session is highly confrontive.

• Students should have the opportunity to take some responsibility for organizing, structuring, and conducting the groups.

• Other than to assure the physical safety of the participants, few group rules should exist.

• The school administration must support the concept of cross-cultural group counseling if it is to be successful. Difficulties and uncertainties that arise from such an undertaking cannot be worked out without this commitment on the part of the administration.

• To foster cooperation, the facilitators of the groups should keep the school administrators informed of developments within the groups. They should also give feedback to faculty on the development and progress of the entire project.

- Discussions do not have to focus exclusively on racial issues. Exploration of values, cultural differences, community considerations, or communication skills are examples of subjects for group discussion that lend themselves well to this kind of experience.
- The group counseling model should be flexible and able to adapt to the changing needs of the students and the school.
- Black and white cofacilitators should be used if at all possible.
- While not desirable, conflict and confrontation often act as catalysts for productive cross-cultural group sessions.
- Values clarification strategies and other human relations training techniques have much potential for cross-cultural groups. One of the major purposes of these groups is to aid individuals to interact positively with racially different people.
- The lower the grade level at which true integration is achieved, the greater the possibility of students being able to experience a feeling of belonging.
- Social events that bring students together outside the school should be encouraged. Interaction in settings other than the classroom or counseling group can increase understanding of other cultures as well as deepen individual insight into and appreciation for one's own cultural background.

APPENDIX A

STUDENT QUESTIONNAIRE

This questionnaire will gather information about the cross-culture discussion groups. Since *you* participated directly in the discussion groups, *your* opinions are of great importance to us. *Please respond to each item.* If you would like to write additional comments, please use the space provided or the back of the sheet. Be honest, direct, and complete. Your suggestions and recommendations for improving the discussion groups are appreciated. Your responses will be kept confidential.

1. Your present grade: (check one)
    [ ] 7   [ ] 8   [ ] 9   [ ] 10
          [ ] 11   [ ] 12

2   Your sex: (check one)
    [ ] Male   [ ] Female

3. Last September at the start of the school year, how did you feel race relations were in the school?
    [ ] Good   [ ] Average   [ ] Poor
    Comments:

4. When you *first heard* that a part of Waterloo would be in the Laboratory School attendance zone, what did you think of the idea?
    [ ]   Thought it was a *good* idea
    [ ]   Thought it was a *bad* idea
    Comments:

5. How do you feel *now* with regard to a part of Waterloo being in the Laboratory School attendance zone?
    [ ]   Think it is a *good* idea
    [ ]   Think it is a *bad* idea
    Comments:

6. How would you rate race relations within the Laboratory School compared to race relations outside of school?
    [ ]   Race relations are *better* in the school.

[ ]   Race relations are *worse* in the school.

[ ]   Race relations are *about the same* in the school and outside of school.

Comments:

7. Do you feel that racial harmony within the school can be achieved by leaving it to the students—that is, the students will naturally achieve this by themselves?

[ ]   Yes   [ ]   No

Comments:

8. Do you feel that cross-cultural discussion groups have a useful part to play in a multiracial school?

[ ]   Yes   [ ]   No

Comments:

9. To what degree have cross-cultural discussion groups in the Laboratory School helped to bring about racial harmony and understanding?

[ ]   The discussions have had a great positive effect on all segments of the student body.

[ ]   The discussion groups have had a great positive effect on those participating in them.

[ ]   The discussion groups have had some positive effect.

[ ]   The discussion groups have had very little effect on anyone.

[ ]   The discussion groups have had a negative effect.

Comments:

10. What is the greatest source of racial disunity in the Laboratory School?

[ ]   Influence of parents

[ ]   Not all students live in the same community

[ ] Possible loss of friendships if seen associating interracially

[ ] Other (specify) ——————————

Comments:

11. To what degree have the counselors (Mr. Brown, Mr. Rainey, Mr. Strub) been sensitive to your ideas?

[ ] Very sensitive

[ ] Moderately sensitive

[ ] Not sensitive

Comments:

12. Do you feel comfortable (at ease) with the counselors?

[ ] Very comfortable

[ ] Moderately comfortable

[ ] Uncomfortable, uneasy

Comments:

13. Do the counselors seem up-to-date?

[ ] Old ideas, old-fashioned

[ ] New ideas, modern

[ ] Flexible points-of-view

Comments:

14. Do you feel that most of the *others* in the cross-cultural discussion groups expressed themselves openly and honestly?

[ ] Very open and honest

[ ] Moderately open and honest

[ ] Held back, faked their real feelings

Comments:

15. Do you feel that *you* expressed yourself openly and honestly in the cross-cultural discussion groups?

[ ] Very open and honest

[ ] Moderately open and honest

[   ]   Held back, kept true feelings to yourself
Comments:

16.   (Black students only. White students should skip this
      item and go on to question 18.)
      Do you feel that most of the *white* students expressed
      themselves openly and honestly in the discussion
      groups?
      [   ]   Very open and honest
      [   ]   Moderately open and honest
      [   ]   Held back, faked their real feelings
      Comments:

17.   (Black students only.) Do you feel that most of the
      black students expressed themselves openly and hon-
      estly in the discussion groups?
      [   ]   Very open and honest
      [   ]   Moderately open and honest
      [   ]   Held back, faked their real feelings
      Comments?

18.   (White students only. Black students should skip this
      item and go on to question 20.)
      Do you feel that most of the *black* students expressed
      themselves openly and honestly in the discussion
      groups?
      [   ]   Very open and honest
      [   ]   Moderately open and honest
      [   ]   Held back, faked their real feelings
      Comments:

19.   (White students only.) Do you feel that most of the
      white students expressed themselves openly and hon-
      estly in the discussion groups?
      [   ]   Very open and honest
      [   ]   Moderately open and honest

[   ]   Held back, faked their real feelings
Comments:

10.   Would you like to participate in a cross-cultural group again?
      [   ]   Yes
      [   ]   No
      Comments:

21.   Do you think there should be cross-cultural discussion groups next year?
      [   ]   Yes
      [   ]   No
      Comments:

22.   Do you feel that other teachers should be involved in the cross-cultural discussion groups?
      [   ]   Yes
      [   ]   No
      Comments:

23.   Do you feel that the principal (Dr. Albrecht) should be involved in the cross-cultural discussion groups?
      [   ]   Yes
      [   ]   No
      Comments:

24.   Since you have been involved in the cross-cultural groups, how has your attitude changed toward fellow students who are racially different from yourself?
      [   ]   More tolerant
      [   ]   Less tolerant
      [   ]   About the same
      Comments:

25.   Do you feel that, without the cross-cultural groups, racial harmony would have

[　] Lessened
[　] Remained as it was
[　] Increased
Comments:

26. How should the cross-cultural groups operate?
    [　] Mostly talk (discussion)
    [　] Mostly other activities. Specify activities
    Comments:

27. What is the *best* feature of the cross-cultural discussion groups as they were conducted this year? (Use the back of this sheet for additional space if needed.)

28. What is the *worst* feature of the cross-cultural discussion groups as they were conducted this year? (Use the back of this sheet for additional space if needed.)

APPENDIX B

FACULTY-ADMINISTRATOR QUESTIONNAIRE

This questionnaire will gather information about the cross-culture discussion groups. Your opinions are of great importance to us. *Please respond to each item.* If you would like to write additional comments, please use the space provided on the back of the sheet. Your suggestions and recommendations for improving the discussion groups are appreciated.

1. Your subject area and grade:

2. How do you feel *now* with regard to a part of Waterloo being in the Laboratory School attendance zone?
   [　] Think it is a *good* idea

[ ] Think it is a *bad* idea
Comments:

3. How would you rate race relations within the Laboratory School compared to race relations outside of school?
[ ] Race relations are *better* in the school.
[ ] Race relations are *worse* in the school.
[ ] Race relations are *about the same* in the school and outside of school.
Comments:

4. Do you feel that racial harmony within the school can be achieved by leaving it to students—that is, the students will naturally achieve this by themselves?
[ ] Yes
[ ] No
Comments:

5. Do you feel that cross-cultural discussion groups have a useful part to play in a multiracial school?
[ ] Yes
[ ] No
Comments:

6. To what degree have cross-cultural discussion groups in the Laboratory School helped to bring about racial harmony and understanding?
[ ] The discussion groups have had a great positive effect on all segments of the student body.
[ ] The discussion groups have had a great positive effect on those participating in them.
[ ] The discussion groups have had some positive effect.
[ ] The discussion groups have had very little effect on anyone.

[ ] The discussion groups have had a negative effect.
Comments:

7. Since the time when cross-cultural group discussion first began, what are your perceptions of attitudinal changes of students toward fellow students who are racially different from themselves?
   [ ] More tolerant
   [ ] Less tolerant
   [ ] About the same
   [ ] Other
   [ ] No response
   Comments:

8. Do you feel that without the cross-cultural group, racial harmony would have
   [ ] Lessened
   [ ] Remained as it was
   [ ] Increased
   Comments:

9. How would you characterize the effect provided by the cross-cultural discussion groups on the degree of communication between black and white students?
   [ ] Strong positive effect
   [ ] Some positive effect
   [ ] No effect
   [ ] Some negative effect
   [ ] Strong negative effect
   Comments:

10. How would you characterize the opportunities provided by the cross-cultural discussion groups for ra-

cially different students to resolve differences by dialogue and discussion?

[ ]   Good opportunity
[ ]   Some opportunity
[ ]   Little opportunity
[ ]   No opportunity
[ ]   Other
Comments:

11. How would you characterize the effect provided by the cross-cultural discussion groups on those students who did not directly participate in them?

[ ]   Strong positive effect
[ ]   Some positive effect
[ ]   No effect
[ ]   Some negative effect
[ ]   Strong negative effect
Comments:

12. What is the greatest source of racial disunity in the Laboratory School?

[ ]   Influence of parents
[ ]   Not all students live in the same community
[ ]   Possible loss of friendship if seen associating interracially
[ ]   Other (specify) ——————
Comments:

13. Do you think there should be cross-cultural discussion groups next year?

[ ]   Yes
[ ]   No
Comments:

14. Do you feel that teachers should be involved in the cross-cultural discussion

[ ]   Yes
[ ]   No
Comments:

APPENDIX C

SELECTED VERBATIM STUDENT COMMENTS TO QUESTIONNAIRE ITEMS

The following comments are representative of written responses students made on the questionnaire. In several instances, individuals made both a written response and checked a response option available to them.

The question itself is listed and followed by some of the comments.

> *Question 7:* Do you feel that racial harmony within the school can be achieved by leaving it to the students—that is, the students will naturally achieve this by themselves?

I don't think the students really can do it themselves but they can achieve it a lot better than adults, who can't do it at all.

Everyone is too afraid of anyone from another race to associate with them, so race relations must be given a push.

For some students yes, for some students no, I mean there is still prejudice and stuff though in our generation it is sort of snuffed out. But some kids need prodding.

If the students want to be friendly they will and if they don't they won't and nothing anybody can say can change their minds.

Question 8: Do you feel that cross-cultural discussion groups have a useful part to play in a multiracial school?

It gives you a chance to ask questions and let your feelings be known. You can find out things you might never have known.

I feel that sometimes in the group the discussions are very good. The problem is, *everything is forgotten until the next meeting in a small classroom.*

Because it helps to find out why the blacks have problems talking to the whites and vice versa. Also where they feel uncomfortable so we can change it to make them comfortable.

I still think it is more good than bad. At least it is a step, it may be reluctant and shaky, but hopefully, some day we can strengthen that step and make it strong and good. That would never happen if we never tried.

Question 14: Do you feel that most of the *others* in the cross-cultural discussion groups expressed themselves openly and honestly?

Most were very open and expressed their feelings. But I got the impression from some that they had to put on a show and agree or disagree instead of saying what he or she felt.

Question 16: (Black students only. White students should skip this item and go on to question 18.) Do you feel that most of the *white* students expressed themselves openly and honestly in the discussion groups?

I don't really know. For some reason I don't think they say what they feel, because as soon as they get in their little groups they go back to the way they were before the meeting.

> *Question 18:* (White students only. Black students should skip this item and go on to question 20.) Do you feel that most of the *black* students expressed themselves openly and honestly in the discussion groups?

I can't answer this. But I must say that it appears that they are not too concerned with showing their feelings unless upon fire from racist whites.

> *Question 19:* (White students only.) Do you feel that most of the *white* students expressed themselves openly and honestly in the discussion groups?

The whites are more aggressive and seem to talk more. They appear to be more sensitive and care about this issue. Except for the racist whites who attack or are apathetic and don't come.

> *Question 20:* Would you like to participate in a cross-cultural group again?

It really sort of depends, because I think it sort of should be a bigger group and with teachers in order to get anything accomplished.

> *Question 24:* Since you have been involved in the cross-cultural groups, how has your attitude changed toward fellow students who are racially different from yourself?

I can't say it changed. I never learned anything or gained any understanding to change it. (Well, I did a little.)

APPENDIX D

SELECTED VERBATIM FACULTY COMMENTS TO QUESTIONNAIRE ITEMS

The following comments are representative of written responses faculty and administrators made on the questionnaire. In several instances individuals made both a written response and checked a response option available to them.

The question itself is listed and followed by some of the comments.

> *Question 4:* Do you feel that racial harmony within the school can be achieved by leaving it to students—that is, the students will naturally achieve this by themselves?

While the ultimate proof will be the kids, it is clear to me that adult intervention, guidance, and shaping will be necessary at every stage of the program. Kids too often don't have the maturity and information needed to solve disagreements themselves.

Certainly this would be true in some situations, and with some students. However, to progress and improve understanding, it cannot be left to chance.

Not as effectively as when all concerned are involved in promoting understanding and harmony.

The students will naturally form into groups. These groups may or may not follow racial boundary lines. If the groups are racial, loyalty owed to the group and racial harmony becomes very difficult.

I think they need some help and guidance because of pressures they may be experiencing at home or in the community.

Not at the secondary level, at least. Parental and peer group influences are too great.

It seems to me that a school is a community of people—the young ones are called students, the old ones are called faculty, but all are people. Racial harmony is a condition among people, all people, and all the people in the community (school) need to be involved, and cooperate, in achieving racial harmony.

Students need to be "pushed" gently into situations within which understanding can be reached.

The students seem to feel this way. I think many white students are more to fault for disharmony than the black students.

True racial harmony will be very difficult to achieve within the school until there is racial harmony within society as a whole. I would expect the racial harmony in school to be more or less dictated by the racial conditions with the community, state, and nation.

Racial harmony must be across faculty-student lines too. Student-student racial harmony must ultimately be achieved by those involved (the students themselves), but the faculty and administration can help create the atmosphere and structure conducive to achievement.

To achieve this social goal requires maturity— and if these students possessed the mature minds needed to achieve this goal, they wouldn't be here in the first place. They definitely need guidance.

Adults influence strongly, children hear and act. There seems to be a wider acceptance all around with smaller kids. Kids learn prejudice from others—most are not "color"conscious till it's pointed out. The younger children, as a group, seem more able to enjoy one another, if left alone. Older kids are more wary than when fewer Waterloo kids were in class. This is for both races. Some say too much was expected and advantages were taken. I really don't know; myself.

But neither can we (the faculty) impose racial harmony. It must be a cooperatively planned and executed action.

May be more true of elementary age; should get better after several years of working with each other through elementary-secondary years.

Discussion groups are extremely important, plus concerted effort by all staff members and students.

Society and the external forces must come into balance before the school will.

Correct societal behavior is learned.

Question 5: Do you feel that cross-cultural discussion groups have a useful part to play in a multiracial school?

In our school it has made a noticeable difference.

It provides an opportunity to express ideas or feelings that may otherwise be repressed and fester if constructive opportunities to develop understandings are not available.

The discussions have probably led to the easing of potential problems.

Let us change the organization, time held, greater involvement of students and teachers.

Airing ideas and grievances often turns out to be nothing more than lack of understanding. But all have to work at it; it is not a one-sided operation with one giving and one taking all the time.

You must communicate.

> *Question 6:* To what degree have cross-cultural discussion groups in the Laboratory School helped to bring about racial harmony and understanding?

The greatest effect has been felt by those participating, but insights gained do transfer to a degree.

I feel the discussion groups were not continued long enough.

I think they have helped "clear the air" at times when tensions were high.

Noticed a lessening of tensions, but unable to determine if cross-cultural discussions helped.

I suspect that what we have is a facade rather than real harmony and understanding.

Question 7: Since the time when cross-cultural group discussions first began, what are your perceptions of attitudinal changes of students toward fellow students who are racially different from themselves?

There is no question that there has been real growth in attitudes and cultural understanding.

There has been a different feeling in the building this year. The atmosphere is more like a feeling that each situation has to be weighed in its own context and judged, rather than an instantaneous reaction by all.

It is conceivable that the students are just getting used to each other but it is likely that the attitudes have been changed faster due to the cross-cultural group discussions.

I see more toleration, but not to the extent the term "more" implies.

Question 10: How would you characterize the opportunities provided by the cross-cultural discussion groups for racially different students to resolve differences by dialogue and discussion?

As I understand it, this has been one of the principal features of the program, and, in my opinion, one of its strengths.

Dialogue is a beginning, the classroom is a continuation of the dialogue.

There have been plenty of opportunities, if that is what is implied.

Question 11: How would you characterize the effect provided by the cross-cultural discussion groups on those students who did not directly participate in them?

The main benefits have been to the participants, but direct feedback to other students, and observation of changed attitudes and behavior has been of value to others.

The greatest effect has been felt by those participating, but insights gained do transfer to a degree.

Question 13: Do you think there should be cross-cultural discussion groups next year?

I encourage the guidance staff and administration to continue the project indefinitely.

No question about this. I do think there should be involvement of more kids. There is a danger of "clubbiness" built into the present structure, it seems to me.

It should be expanded to include more students and a greater cross-section of the student body.

But I'm not sure they should be called cross-cultural. Perhaps what we need is sensitivity training.

Again, I do not know what effects, positive or negative, the discussion groups have had, but they appear to be one method of getting problems into the open.

As long as students feel there is value in them.

If we have the commitment to this program that we claim we have, then there ought to be some means found to involve all of our students in this program and without taking them out of academic classes—perhaps we could substitute cross-cultural groups for the lounge periods. When students are taken out of regularly scheduled classes, you are depriving them of equal educational opportunities. Furthermore, when you fail to involve all students in the cross-cultural groups, you are still depriving them of equal opportunities—you are lucky someone hasn't filed a court suit against you. Furthermore, to take students out of a teacher's class is a violation of the school's contractual obligation with that individual teacher.

REFERENCES

Albrecht, J. E. Why integrated education. *A Challenge Change,* March 1972, p. 2.

Brunner, J. S. The process of education revisited. *Phi Delta Kappan,* September 1971, p. 21.

Campbell, J. D., & Yarrow, M. Personal and situational variables in adaptation to change. *Journal of Social Issues,* 1958, *14,* 29–46.

Carkhuff, R. R., & Banks, G. Training as a preferred mode of facilitating relations between races and generations. *Journal of Counseling Psychology,* 1970, *17,* 413–418.

Chesler, M., Jorgensen, C., & Erenberg, P. *Planning educational change: Integrating the desegregated school.* Ann Arbor, Michigan: Center for Research on Utilization of Scientific Knowledge, 1970. (ERIC Document Reproduction Service No. ED 042071.)

Costin, F. Behavioral and attitudinal changes resulting from an intergroup youth project. *The Journal of Intergroup Relations,* 1966, *5,* 53–64.

Cottle, T. J. Encounter in color. *Psychology Today,* December 1967, p. 22.

Erickson, E. H. The concept of identity in race relations: Notes and queries. *Daedalus,* Winter, 1966, pp. 145–171.

Green, R. L., Smith, E., & Schweitzer, J. H. Bussing and the multiracial classroom. *Phi Delta Kappan,* May 1972, p. 546.

Hansen, L. S., & Wirgau, O. Human relations training: A response to crisis. *The School Counselor,* 1970, *17,* 253–257.

Hartoonian, M. H., & Risberg, D. An approach to human relations education. *Newsletter,* 1971, *24,* 15–19.

Howard, R. C. A descriptive analysis of verbal interaction in a biracial counseling group of college undergraduates. Unpublished doctoral dissertation, University of South Dakota, 1970.

Kranz, P. L. The wound that heals. *Civil Rights Digest,* 1972, *5,* 29–36.

McArdle, C., & Young, N. F. Classroom discussion on identity or how can we make it without "acting white." *American Journal of Orthopsychiatry,* 1970, *40,* 135–141.

Meyers, D. G., & Bishop, G. D. Discussion effects on racial attitudes. *Science,* 1970, *169,* 778–779.

Middleman, R. R. On being a whitey in the midst of a racial crisis. *Children,* 1969, *16,* 97–102.

Moore, R. E. *The human side of successful communication.* Englewood Cliffs, New Jersey: Prentice Hall, 1961.

Owens, I. *The effect of group leader(s) race on group counseling undertaken to improve inter-group attitude among racially mixed fifth and sixth grade children.* Morgertown, W. V.: West Virginia University, 1969. (ERIC Document Reproduction Service No. ED 041328.)

Pettigrew, T. Social psychology and desegregation report. *American Psychologist,* 1961, *16,* 105–112.

Powell, J. H. *Interim report of the Institute for Supervision of Student Teachers on problems occasioned by desegregation of public schools.* Lexington, Kentucky: Kentucky University, 1965. (ERIC Document Reproduction Service No. ED 045742.)

Ramirez, M., III. *Value conflicts experienced by Mexican-American students.* Author, 1968. (ERIC Document Reproduction Service No. ED 059829.)

Richardson, D. O. Use of small group confrontations for changing attitudes between ethnic groups in a senior high school. Unpublished doctoral dissertation, Washington State University, 1969.

Rousseve, R. J. Social hypocrisy and the promises of integrated education. *Integrated Education,* November-December, 1969, p. 44.

Shearouse, H. S. *Inservice education to solve problems incident to the elimination of the dual school system. Final technical report.* Conyers, Georgia: Rockdale County Public Schools, 1969. (ERIC Document Reproduction Service No. ED 045748.)

Singer, D. The impact of interracial classroom exposure on the social attitudes of fifth grade children. Unpublished study, New York University, 1964.

Venditti, F. P. *Program director's manual for solving multi-ethnic problems: A simulation game for elementary and high school teachers.* Knoxville, Tennessee: Tennessee University, 1970. (ERIC Document Reproduction Service No. ED 044465.)

Webster, S. The influence of interracial contact on social acceptance in a newly integrated school. *Journal of Educational Psychology,* 1961, *52,* 769–783.

Weinberg, C. *Social foundations of educational guidance.* New York: The Free Press, 1969.

Willmus, H. G. Behavioral interactions of black and white students in a suburban high school. Unpublished doctoral dissertation, Wisconsin State University, 1972.

Chapter 7

EXEMPLARY PROGRAMS, PRACTICES, AND POLICIES

Carol K. Jaslow

Widespread desegregation efforts are causing an increasing number of schools to become racially heterogeneous. As a result, school personnel, students, counselor educators, and communities need to develop skills in working with minority groups. To this end, governmental policies and guidelines have been established to promote programs and practices that will help effect harmonious relationships for all concerned. On their own initiative, schools have undertaken programs designed to ease the implementation of desegregation and to facilitate the awareness and acceptance of minority cultures. This chapter examines several exemplary efforts—a state-mandated policy established and carried out in Maryland, the comprehensive federally funded Center/Satellite Projects implemented regionally, an attempt by one university to respond to the particular needs of its minority students, and an approach to transcultural counseling from "the other side of the fence."

According to popular theory, the Colonel's Lady and Rosie O'Grady are sisters under the skin, but in the reality of everyday living it just isn't so. Each reflects the characteristics and behaviors assimilated during a lifetime of widely differentiated development.

So it is with the ethnically different. Each group has been nurtured in an environment unique in its culture and mores. For most, the only common denominator is the school. Here all Americans are presumed to be equal, and, as such, are expected to conform to the existing mold. Many don't, won't, or can't fit. Society, and particularly the schools, are fortunately becoming increasingly cognizant of and sympathetic to the need for change. We are recognizing that to be different is not only acceptable but desirable. We are coming to grips with the need not only to understand and appreciate our different youngsters, but to help them on their terms rather than on ours.

School personnel in general and counselors in particular are trying to learn more about the uniqueness of the subcultures with whom they work. From these learning efforts have emerged a number of specialized programs designed to create awareness and acceptance of cultural differences, to build self-esteem and self-acceptance among the ethnically different, and to help counselors and counselor trainees to work more effectively with their subculture clientele.

Good counseling programs are usually the result of many-faceted efforts. Frequently they reflect policies made not only in a single school system but also at district, state, and/or federal levels. This chapter looks at exemplary efforts that have been implemented at each of these levels, with a view toward illustrating not only what can be done but what has been and is being done.

STATE LEVEL

When one thinks of transcultural counseling, one usually envisions work among youngsters in newly integrated public school systems. Although this type of desegregation counseling among majority as well as minority students is not only highly prevalent but necessary, it is by no means the only setting for such efforts. Because desegregation is also a desired target at the college level, there is a great need for secondary school counselors who are skilled in working with potential college applicants with a minority race background. And because there are not enough minority group counselors to serve this ever growing segment of our youth, it is apparent that *all* helping professionals must be sensitized to working with minority-group clients.

To desegregate institutions of higher education, the State of Maryland, in 1974, established an "Inter-Agency Task Force, under the direction of the Maryland Council for Higher Education, in cooperation with the State Department of Education, whose responsibility [was] to promulgate guidelines and procedures to facilitate counseling services for minority group students in secondary schools that [would] maximize 'other-race' application patterns among the colleges" (Inter-Agency, 1974).

Clarifying its intent to encourage minority students to attend predominantly white institutions of higher learning, and whites to attend predominantly black institutions, the Task Force set out to encourage a high school climate conducive to such application. Four regional workshops for black and white secondary school counselors were held throughout the state to provide training in minority group counseling. Emphasis was placed on changing and modifying counselor attitudes toward cultural and racial differences—particularly with respect to family, religion, social relationships, and educational objectives.

Recognizing that they were perhaps putting the cart before the horse by working with counselors already certified, the Task Force also sought to encourage all state colleges which offered programs leading to state certification in guidance and counseling to include, in their preparatory coursework, training in minority group counseling. As of the winter of 1976, all such programs in Maryland except the one at the University of Maryland offered such a course as part of their certification requirements. As these recently certified guidance counselors work in the school systems of Maryland, with their heightened awareness of and sensitivity to the cultural needs of minority students, it is hoped that they will help create a high school climate that will build intragroup identity while breaking down intergroup hostility so that the state goal of "maximizing 'other-race' application patterns" among state colleges will be realized.

As a second prong to this attack on "single-race" college enrollment, the state has recently embarked on a new program which operates through all secondary schools and is designed to reach each and every eleventh and twelfth grader in the schools, regardless of post-high-school plans. An attractive brochure lists all state institutions of higher learning; but instead of dividing them according to geographical region, community size, student body composition, etc., the brochure organizes them by program offerings and includes all colleges and universities in Maryland, regardless of racial composition, in the appropriate programmatic categories. Included in each booklet is a stamped card which students may use to request further information about any college. It is hoped that this counselor's tool will relieve secondary school counselors of the burden of reaching all potential college students with appropriate and sufficient information, and especially those students for whom college had not previously been an option. The return cards will also give the students themselves some sense of control over their own lives by allowing them to assume a measure of responsibility for obtaining information. It is anticipated that use of the brochure, with its emphasis on programs rather than institutions, will dramatically encourage both white and minority group students to seek admission to "other-race" colleges and universities in Maryland.

FEDERAL LEVEL

Realizing that good counseling starts with the counselor rather than the program, the federal government authorized what surely has been one of the most ambitious minority personnel development programs ever undertaken. Funded under Public Law 90-35, the Education Professions Development Act (EPDA), the Center/Satellite Pupil Personnel Services (PPS) Project Program was launched in 1971 for a period of 3 years. Seven selected universities around the country were chosen to serve as "centers" for the program in their areas; additional colleges or communities within their geographical sphere were selected as "satellites" working with the center facility to develop, utilize, and evaluate counselor training programs specifically geared to the minority populations in the regions served by their institutions.

The general objective of each center was the development of a corp of personnel workers specifically trained to work with minority group clients. Program design and implementation were largely left to the individual centers. Within each center/satellite grouping, a greater measure of autonomy prevailed so that each satellite, working closely with its center institution, could respond to the concerns of its particular population group. Seven such centers were established, speaking to the needs of American Indians, Asian Americans, blacks, and Chicanos. Obviously not all minority groups in the nation were covered by this project. Groups greatly underrepresented by appropriate minority counseling personnel, vis-à-vis their client population, were the primary target populations for the program.

Southeastern Regional EPDA-PPS Center/Satellite Project

Experience has indicated that black clients, like other minority ethnic groups, generally relate more readily to other blacks than to whites (Katz, 1963). The difficulties in a black client–white counselor relationship are often caused by language ambiguities, feelings of being patronized or denigrated on the part of the minority person, and general distrust by both parties. American blacks are reluctant "disclosers," especially to whites whom they do not feel they can trust. In particular, this fear of disclosing comes from a fear of being "understood," which in turn results in a perceived loss of autonomy and control (Vontress, 1972). Such concerns obviously are counterproductive to a counseling relationship and attest to the great need for more black counselors who can relate to blacks in a nonthreatening way.

However this paucity of black teachers and counselors means that black youngsters, particularly those from the inner city, have a difficult time fitting into an environment where so few speak their language. So many drop out that in cities like Philadelphia and Louisville an inner city youngster entering junior high school stands only a 40% chance of completing high school (Final Program Report, 1975). Those who remain often become involved in delinquent behavior, both in and out of school. Learning gets left behind when school personnel have to spend their time and energy on discipline.

In response to these long-standing problems, several center/satellite projects have directed their efforts toward upgrading services to inner city schools and youngsters. One such program is centered in Nashville, Tennessee. It is coordinated jointly by Tennessee State University and the University of Tennessee, the former serving primarily black students and the latter serving primarily white students.

The satellite institutions in this program were paired in black/white dyads, as were the centers in Nashville. This pairing demonstrated the desire on the part of both administrations to improve the relations not only between the black/white institutions but also among the black/white community in general. The Southeastern Regional Center/Satellite Project pairings included Jackson State College and the University of Mississippi, Georgia State University and Atlanta University, Alabama State University and the University of Alabama, and Florida State University and Florida A&M.

The general objectives of the program were similar to those for all the programs: (1) to improve the qualifications of both trainers and supervisors of pupil personnel specialists; (2) to work cooperatively with schools and related community agencies to train pupil personnel specialists and school staff to function effectively as teams; (3) to design, implement, and evaluate programs appropriate for low-income area schools; (4) to recruit and train members of minority groups and individuals who work with them as pupil personnel specialists; and (5) to effect organizational change in the teaching institutions and in the schools to facilitate achievement of the stated goals.

Part of the thrust of this center/satellite project was to help urban teachers improve the classroom climate in schools which, because of recently implemented integration moves, had experienced large racial shifts of both students and teachers. Meeting these goals called for the collaboration of pupil personnel staff, instructional staff, school and community resources, and parents. This effort focused on the development of interpersonal skills and behaviors; the modification of curricula to meet the needs of the students more adequately, with emphasis on transcultural understanding; and the improvement of home-school liaisons wherein parents, students, and staff could share in goal setting and decision making relative to the educational process.

A second thrust of the Southeastern Regional Project was directed toward those satellites paired to work together to improve their programs of counselor education. The goals for these institutions were establishing a long-term working relationship with their co-institution, designing and testing new models of counselor training, and providing consultant teams to work with a sample of target area children and their parents. (Southeastern EPDA-PPS Center/Satellite Project, Tennessee State University and the University of Tennessee, Nashville, TN. Director: George W. Cox)

Northeastern EPDA-PPS Center/Satellite Project

A second center/satellite project which attempted to improve educational climates, particularly for black youngsters, was the Northeastern Center/Satellite Project at the University of Pittsburgh. General objectives for the project again were similar to those for other projects—to improve training programs for pupil personnel workers; to train people to create better learning environments for students; to establish effective liaison between school personnel and the community; and to encourage pupil personnel workers to work with educational and social systems, as well as with individual clients. This project, in response to existing community conditions, included an additional dimension —establishment and implementation of field experiences in such alternative institutions as free schools and free clinics. This move resulted from two factors: (1) the need for certified personnel in these nontraditional settings, and (2) the urging of urban minority groups, particularly blacks, for better response to their needs (McGreevy, 1973).

Most of the satellites in the Northeastern Project devoted efforts to training classroom teachers as trainees, counselors, consultants, and change agents—not only for individual students, but also for local school systems. The satellite at Boston University, however, sought a more comprehensive approach by including in its training not only graduate students in counselor education but also nurses in graduate nursing programs, upper-level psychiatric residents, and graduate students in social work. From this group of trainees it sent teams to work as change agents in selected inner city schools. It should be remembered that one goal of all the center/satellite projects was to create a "new professional" in the area of pupil personnel specialists, and to establish career ladders in the community up which trainees might advance. Universities participating in the Northeastern Regional Project included Duquesne University at Pittsburgh, Howard University at Washington, D.C., SUNY at Buffalo and at Brockport, and Boston University. (Northeastern EPDA-PPS Center/Satellite Project, University of Pittsburgh, PA. Co-Directors: Joel Welinick and Wilma Smith)

Midwest EPDA-PPS Center/Satellite Project

The Northeastern Regional Project was not the only one directed primarily to inner city blacks. The Midwest Center was also targeted toward this population. Satellite institutions affiliated with the EPDA Midwest Center Consortium were the Universities of Illinois at Chicago and Urbana, Indiana University at Bloomington, University of Louisville, and the Ohio State University at Columbus. Although the program focused primarily on inner city minority students, the individual satellites in this program functioned in varied and autonomous, albeit coordinated, ways.

All satellites sought to implement changes in the organizational structure of the school or school system with which they worked, as well as in the curriculum structure of the university training program with which they were affiliated. Whereas most of the satellites attempted to improve the quality of training for pupil personnel workers, one focused its attention on retraining teachers and other school staff, and one sought to train a new kind of school social worker who would try to upgrade the way in which school systems respond to children, particularly minority group children.

Each center collaborated with a nearby urban school district for interactive change, wherein new trainees upgraded the level of services offered to minority children in the schools while program design at the training institutions concurrently became more realistic.

Several outcomes were apparent as a result of this center/satellite program: (1) successful efforts to improve the training curriculum at the universities, making it reality- and experientially-oriented; (2) greater sensitivity and responsiveness to the needs of inner city minority youngsters; (3) greater involvement of parents and community in decision making affecting the schools; and (4) development and field testing of new techniques of teaching, counseling, and interacting. (Midwest EPDA-PPS Center/Satellite Project, Indiana University, Bloomington, IN. Director: DeWayne J. Kurpius)

Southwestern EPDA-PPS Center/Satellite Project

All ethnic groups have differences which set them apart from each other and from the American Caucasian majority. Those white ethnic groups that do not differ visibly from mainstream whites and who have, over the years, given up those cultural factors that distinguish them have become largely assimilated. However, many ethnic groups choose not to assimilate or are unable to do so because of a number of factors. For whatever reasons, large segments of our population still form highly visible, culturally different groups whose needs are uniquely different from those of the assimilated majority.

Mexican Americans, for example, generally live together in large numbers, isolated in barrios. There is little need for many of them to speak English, except in the schools. The children therefore find it difficult if not impossible to communicate with Anglos at school, and their silence or misunderstood responses often cause them to be labeled "slow." Sometimes youngsters who can speak English choose not to, as one way of maintaining their privacy. Machismo is a characteristic inherent in Hispanic males and must be accepted and dealt with by Anglos seeking to work with them in a helping relationship (Vontress, 1972). Suspicion also looms large in Hispanic cultural mores and causes them to be wary of those who are trying to help them.

Schools of the southwest have chronically suffered a shortage of counselors, particularly Chicanos. Of the 3388 counselors in the region, only 184 are Chicano. Although the overall pupil/counselor ratio is 1124:1, in districts 10% or more Mexican American the ratio of Mexican American pupils to counselors is 1926:1 (USCCR Survey, 1969). Such a serious lack means that most Chicano youngsters who need someone to talk to are denied a "sympatico" relationship with a Chicano counselor.

To alleviate this situation, a center/satellite project was established with its nucleus at the University of New Mexico at Albuquerque, the heart of the nation's greatest concentration of Mexican Americans. Its thrust was twofold: (1) to bring about organizational change in those institutions that trained and employed pupil personnel specialists to work with Hispanic Americans, and (2) to train graduate level pupil personnel specialists to work with Spanish-speaking students. The program was centered at the University of New Mexico, where most of the training of pupil personnel specialists and development of pupil personnel services took place.

Satellite institutions involved in the Southwestern Region included the University of Colorado at Boulder, Arizona State University at Tempe, Fresno (California) State University, San Diego State University, and the El Paso (Texas) Public Schools. Persons selected by each satellite for graduate training at the center were both bilingual and bicultural, already experienced, and working in target area schools. Following training they were expected to return to their school systems in leadership positions to consult with administrators and teachers, to coordinate school and community related programs, and to counsel students and their families (Rinaldi, 1974).

The training program at the center included courses in Mexican American education to create awareness of the problems of the Chicano youngsters in schools, to analyze regional differences and similarities of Mexican American students in the Southwest, and to discuss acculturation among Chicanos (Aleman, 1974). The training program also addressed itself to strategies to enable program graduates to effect organizational change in the educational communities in which they would later function. Following 2-1/2 semesters of training at the center, students in the program returned to their satellites for field experience in target schools or community agencies. After graduation from the program, more than 50 Chicano pupil personnel specialists were placed in schools, colleges, and community agencies (Rinaldi, 1974). (Southwestern EPDA-PPS Center/Satellite Project, University of New Mexico, Albuquerque, NM. Co-Directors: John R. Rinaldi and Guy W. Trujillo)

Texas EPDA-PPS Center/Satellite Project

A second project geared to the improvement of educational services to the Mexican American community, the Texas Center/Satellite Project, has given its primary attention to four areas in the state with particularly high concentrations of disadvantaged Chicanos—Lubbock, San Angelo, San Antonio, and the South Texas Valley. Initially located at the Texas Technical University in Lubbock, the Center for this project moved, in its second year, to Pan

American University near Corpus Christi. Other institutions of higher education involved in the project were San Angelo State University, Our Lady of the Lake College at San Antonio, and Texas Technical University at Lubbock. Component groups involved intimately with the satellite institutions were, first and foremost, the local Chicano communities, the Intermediate School Districts, and the Regional Education Service Centers of the State Education Agency. In addition, liaisons were established with the state guidance division and with agencies in the community such as crisis and drug centers.

An overriding assumption of the Texas program was that change is inevitable and ongoing, and as such it should be planned and controlled. A strong component of the program was to work with the schools and communities in each Satellite area to develop "an attitude of willingness to change" (Texas Center, 1973). This focus derived from the need to build into the program the mechanisms for maintenance and self-correction following termination of federal funding.

The program placed strong emphasis on the child and his environments—the home, school, and community. Chicano students in the target areas were dropping out of school far more frequently than their Anglo counterparts, their achievement levels were much lower, and of those who were qualified to seek a college education, the percentage of those who actually did was far below that among Anglos. To help effect change, the program sought to stress a developmental rather than a remedial approach to student services; to orient its components to the changing needs of the community; to encourage open communication and collaboration between various school constituencies including teachers, administrators, students, and parents; to sensitize the constituencies to Mexican-American culture; to create a student-centered classroom environment with emphasis on development and creativity; and to encourage parents to become decision-making partners in the education of their children.

A second direction of the program involved changing the counselor training programs at the colleges and universities in the satellite clusters, to make them more experiential, humanistic, ethnically aware, and competency-based. It was anticipated that ripple effects from such changes would reach other counselor education programs in the satellite areas, providing them with an understanding of the need for as well as impetus toward effective change in their institutions.

Training for the Texas project was implemented among four levels of trainees: (1) counselor-certified participants training to become change agents; (2) counselors and recent graduates of counselor education programs to improve interpersonal skills; (3) school administrators to develop an acceptance of the need for change, to acquire team-building skills, and to develop a collaborative process; and (4) district and college level administrators to become acquainted with the total training program, with the need for planned change, and with the understanding of what project-trained counselors would be capable of doing when they returned to their districts.

As the project advanced through its third funded year, it sought to implement, in a variety of settings, revised versions of the models that had been shown to be most effective in previous years. Following the third project year, those models that proved most successful during the previous 2 years were implemented in large city schools with the goal of their becoming permanent components of the satellite school systems. As in all the center/satellite projects, it was hoped that the local school districts would continue to support the programs which brought greatly expanded services not only to the students but to the staff, parents, and community at large. (Texas EPDA-PPS Center/Satellite Project, Pan American University, Edinburg, TX. Co-

Directors: Louis Casaus, George Smith and Miguel Martinez)

California EPDA-PPS Center/Satellite Project

Asian Americans who number about 1-1/2 million form another highly visible and very distinct ethnic group. Although several personality characteristics of this population may be very difficult for others to comprehend, they must be acknowledged and accepted by non-Orientals who are trying to help Asian Americans. At the core of the Asian American personality—particularly among Japanese Americans who constitute the largest subgroup of American Orientals—there is the need to maintain an essence of order, obedience, and conformity (Meredith, 1966). Asian Americans meet these needs in several basic and specific ways: (1) self-denigration to ward off envy; (2) social conformity to prevent shame, especially to the family; and (3) modesty and reserve as respect for authority. We have already noted historical and cultural differences which make it particularly difficult for Anglos to be effective in helping roles with blacks; the situation is no different vis-à-vis Asian Americans.

Whereas several EPDA projects focused specifically on blacks and hispanic Americans, only one concerned itself additionally with Asian Americans. The California Center/Satellite Project at California State University, Hayward, sought to effect institutional changes in pupil personnel training programs with the hope of eventually changing schools and school systems, making them better able to serve Third World students and their communities. This project was initiated through a summer workshop which included Asian, black, and Chicano students from school psychology and counseling and school social work, as well as faculty, representatives from the local schools, school administrators, and community representatives. A heavy emphasis in the center/satellite project was to create permanent mechanisms which would ensure leadership training and employability of Third World graduate students in high-level leadership positions—goals which were, in fact, accomplished. Several satellites pledged to help place their graduates in their affiliate school districts. (Similar attempts to place graduates were actually made by most of the EPDA Projects.)

In other major respects the California project operated in ways quite similar to other projects, wherein University departments worked with local schools to prepare pupil personnel specialists to serve minority group youngsters and their communities.

Satellite institutions participating in the California project were the University of California at Berkeley and the California State Universities at San Jose, Hayward, and San Francisco. (Stanford University participated for the first year but was not refunded.) (California EPDA-PPS Center/Satellite Project, California State University, Hayward, CA. Director: Alvin H. Jones, Jr.)

Northwestern EPDA-PPS Center/Satellite Project

American Indians are one of the most sorely underrepresented minority groups in our nation in the helping professions. Of the more than half million Indians in the country, between 300,000 and 400,000 live on reservations while the rest have attempted assimilation in the cities. Non-Indian counselors trying to work among Indians, particularly those on reservations, face many difficulties directly related to culture. In addition to the language barrier (English-speaking vs. non-English-speaking, abstract vs. concrete reasoning, verbal fluency vs. taciturnity), Indians tend to be suspicious of those Indians and non-Indians whom they perceive as being better than they are. They resist outside attempts to help them upgrade themselves academically or financially, lest it be thought they are trying to be better than their peers (Vontress, 1972). Since non-Indians often find it difficult to empathize fully with cultural values so often at odds with their own, they encounter problems in trying to serve in a helping role. This difficulty makes it apparent that a sizable corps of Indian personnel workers must be developed to serve the needs of their peers.

The only EPDA Program designed to train American Indians to work as counselors for American Indians, the program centered at the University of South Dakota at Vermillion had three general objectives: (1) to establish career ladders to enable low-income persons to move through a graduate program in personnel services and to become eligible for employment as counselors, supervisors, and trainers of additional personnel service workers from the target population; (2) to involve the target communities as well as professional educators and trainees in decision making in order to revamp the counseling curriculum to make it more responsive to those special groups it sought to serve; and (3) to act as change agents in the target school systems so that the systems themselves would become more responsive to the needs of their students.

Satellites affiliated with the University of South Dakota were Eastern Washington State College at Cheney, the University of Montana at Missoula, the University of Wyoming at Laramie, and the University of North Dakota at Grand Forks. Each satellite had its own advisory board and director and its own target schools which provided 9-week field placement opportunities for the trainees. All trainees were of Indian descent and were committed to the field experience internship in a school system in the reservation area. Trainees received a stipend plus tuition and fees.

One direct result of the program has been a series of changes in the counselor education program, which was moved from a primarily didactic to an experiential approach with internships now being integral program components. In its first year the Northwestern Center/Satellite Project produced more Indian guidance and counseling graduates than had been produced in the entire history of the region. As was intended by the program objectives, these personnel workers are working in Indian communities to help today's Indian youth meet tomorrow's challenges. (Northwestern EPDA-PPS Center/Satellite Project, University of South Dakota, Vermillion, SD. Co-Directors: Eric LaPointe and Joe Dupris)

SCHOOL DISTRICT LEVEL

When the Majority is the Minority

When is the majority the minority? When it finds itself transported, in small numbers, into the midst of another culture. This happens when people travel not only to other parts of our country but to other parts of the world. When travel is of short duration, the need for acclimatizing is minimal and temporary. However, when travel results in long-term residence within another cultural milieu, the need for understanding, accepting, and interacting with the host culture becomes a virtual necessity.

Such a situation exists in overseas military service where families are moved for several years. Although they often live in their own communities, shop in their own stores, and attend their own schools, they certainly have contact with the local population, by choice and/or necessity. What a golden opportunity to learn about each other!

One localized but highly ambitious program designed to encourage such cultural awareness among junior high school military dependents has been implemented at a United States dependent school in Puerto Rico. The 60-

hour course was designed to help students develop an understanding and acceptance of cultural pluralism and to acquire enough knowledge of language and culture-specific areas to increase their involvement and effective participation in the Puerto Rican culture (Naval Station, 1974). Students assumed responsibility for their learning, which was largely experiential. Each of the aforementioned goals incorporated specific objectives, which were primarily behavioral. Emphasis was placed on verbal as well as nonverbal communication to teach students that specific behaviors and words have different meanings in the two cultures.

Students were exposed to social conditioning experiments to help them become aware of how cultural conditioning provides a backdrop for our perceptions. Elementary Spanish-language expressions were incorporated into the course with the hope that some knowledge of Spanish could go a long way toward helping students feel at ease with the indigenous population, thereby opening doors of learning and experiencing which would otherwise have remained closed to them. Role-playing techniques encouraged students to use their limited knowledge of language and customs in everyday situations and prepared them for actual mini-field trips to such places as the grocery store, bus stop, record store, or a local restaurant. Regular classroom visits and presentations by a Host National (local resident) exposed students to the spoken language and to social customs and manners from the Puerto Rican viewpoint.

The basic premise of the course was that, since all people do not think and act alike under similar circumstances, and since such differences do not make one set of behaviors right and one wrong, everyone should try harder to familiarize himself with what makes other people tick. In this way people can learn from each other and participate in a mutual exchange.

SINGLE-INSTITUTION LEVEL

Not all programs are extensive and elaborate. Not all are funded by the government. Many are designed and implemented to meet specific needs in specific settings. Sometimes they can be replicated with other groups in other places; sometimes they cannot. One program developed to meet a specific client need in a specific educational environment could, with some revision, be replicated in other settings with other populations.

Minority Student Peer Counseling

Because minority students constituted 20% of the campus student body, yet were very poorly represented among those utilizing clinic services, the staff at the UCLA Student Health Psychiatric Clinic decided to investigate. Since it would have been utopian to speculate that these students did not suffer emotional and psychological problems similar to Caucasians, they determined that there must be other explanations for the problems.

To stimulate use of the clinic facilities by minorities on campus, the clinic staff met with the directors of the four ethnic study programs at UCLA (American Indian, Asian American, black, and Chicano) to determine possible reasons for the reluctance to seek help on the part of their students, and ways to overcome such reluctance. Consensus led to several generalizations: (1) minorities had difficulties relating to white therapists; (2) minorities considered the clinic, as well as the University in general, a white middle-class institution not interested in their concerns; and (3) minorities believed that white therapists would attempt not to help them achieve ethnic identity, but to mold them to conform to the majority middle class (Sue, 1972).

The directors and clinic staff suggested establishing a program to train student volunteers from the four ethnic groups to serve as potential para-professional counselors to minority students who wished to consult a counselor of their own race. Twice as many students volunteered for the training sessions as had been projected (80 vs. 40), which pleased and surprised the staff. Twenty were to be selected to serve as peer counselors following completion of the course.

The class was to focus on the development of interpersonal skills, but the group, hostile to what they perceived as another institutional attempt to mold them, demanded several changes in the class structure. As a compromise the students accepted the need for skill development and the staff offered to provide exposure to campus services such as financial, tutorial, and health facilities.

As class sessions progressed, encounter sessions proved most stimulating, with the general focus being on the development of skills similar to Carkhuff's facilitative and action conditions. The participants came to realize how their own biases affected the counseling process and outcome, and that minority status was not in itself enough to ensure effective counseling.

As a final step in the program, students in each small group were asked to select the five group members who would make the best counselors. Selections by staff and students were amazingly congruent. Twenty para-professionals were selected, as had been initially planned. The program was considered quite successful in that a number of students became counselors on the campus. It was anticipated that the courses in minority student peer counseling would become part of an ongoing program to provide *all* students with adequate campus services.

SUMMARY

With increased emphasis on school integration and the special needs of minority youngsters, particularly in integrated school environments, governmental units as well as training institutions, school districts, and local communities have accepted the need for extensive changes in the delivery of helping services. From the establishment of policies at the federal and state levels, down to school district and community levels, a wide variety of programs are attempting to respond to these changes. This chapter has examined a sampling of what has been and is being done. It discusses some rather elaborate efforts of the federal government through the Education Professions Development Act (EPDA) Pupil Personnel Services (PPS) guidelines, under whose auspices the center/satellite projects were developed; the attempt of one state, Maryland, to equalize the opportunities for all students to enter any state college or university; the program developed by a school district in Puerto Rico, which views transcultural counseling from a very different vantage point; and the successful programmatic effort in a single institution.

Needless to say, much remains to be done. This chapter has attempted to show that changes can be developed and implemented, even in a single school. With federal funding no longer as readily available as in previous years, future change may well have to come through the local schools and school districts.

Changes have to start with people—people with ideas that work for them in their settings. Once people accept the premise that change is inevitable and controllable, they will be in positions to help their institutions and communities develop and implement programs that can lead to greatly improved educational climates for their students, teachers, parents, and community.

REFERENCES

A Final Program Report from Louisville Public Schools and the University of Louisville, 1971–74. Midwest Center/Consortium for Planned

Change in Pupil Personnel Programs for Urban Schools, Bloomington, Indiana, 1975.

Aleman, R. Chicano counselor training: Curriculum and beyond curriculum. Presented at the American Personnel and Guidance Association Convention, New Orleans, Louisiana, April 1974.

Inter-Agency Task Force, Maryland Council for Higher Education and
Maryland State Department of Education. *The articulation of college
guidance for minority and 'other-race' students in secondary and postsecondary
education.* Author, 1974.

Kátz, R. L. *Empathy.* Glencoe, IL: Free Press of Glencoe, 1963.

LaPointe, E. & Twiss, M. *Center satellite program: An Indian counselor training
program.* Vermillion: South Dakota University, School of Education,
1972.

McGreevy, P. (Ed.). *Historical developments of the education professions development act pupil personnel services center/satellite program. Report #1.* USOE,
Grant #OEG-0-70-2021 (725), Washington, D.C.: U.S. Govern-
ment Printing Office, 1973.

Meredith, G. M. Amae and acculturation among Japanese-American
college students in Hawaii. *Journal of Social Psychology,* 1966, *70,*
171–180.

Naval Station Roosevelt Road Human Resource Management Department and Antilles Consolidated Schools. *Cultural awareness: Learning
your way around a new culture.* San Juan, Puerto Rico: Author, 1974.

Rinaldi, J. R. *Graduate programs for Spanish-speaking Americans in pupil personnel services.* Presented at the American College Personnel Association Convention, Chicago, Illinois, April 1974.

Smith, G. *Texas Center/Satellite Project: An Overview.* Edinburg, Texas, Pan
American University 1973.

Sue, S. The training of "third world" students to function as counselors.
Presented at the Western Psychological Association Meeting, Port-
land, Oregon, April 1972.

United States Commission on Civil Rights Survey. Washington, D.C., Spring
1969.

Vontress, C. Counseling racial and ethnic minorities in the United
States. Presented at the American Personnel and Guidance Association Convention, Chicago, Illinois, March 1972.